MYTHOLOGY OF VISHNU AND HIS INCARNATIONS

MYTHOLOGY OF VISHNU AND HIS INCARNATIONS

M.L. Varadpande

GYAN

Mythology of Vishnu and His Incarnations

Rs. 690

ISBN: 978-81-212-1016-4

Published in 2009 in India by
Gyan Publishing House,
23, Main Ansari Road, Darya Ganj,
New Delhi-110002
Phones : 23282060, 23261060
Fax : 011-23285914
E-mail: books@gyanbooks.com
Website: www.gyanbooks.com

Lasser Type Setting by: Quick Media, Delhi
Printed at : Young Art Press, Delhi - 92

Akashat patitam toyam
yatha gacchati sagaram;
Sarva-deva-namaskarah
Keshavam pratigacchati!

Just as water falling from the sky
ultimately reaches the sea, salutations offered
to all the deities ultimately reach
Keshava (Vishnu) alone!

CONTENTS

INTRODUCTION

Vishnu is a major god of Indian pantheon whose roots are found in most ancient of Indian scriptures, the Rig Veda. He is at the centre of vast mythology through his manifold incarnations. Two major epics of India, the Ramayana and the Mahabharata are woven around his two most significant incarnations, Dasharathi Rama and Vasudeva Krishna. His ten incarnations are considered most prominent but there are number of Indian divinities who are connected with him such as Lord Jagannatha of Puri, Vithoba of Pandharpur, Balaji of Giri are considered as his incarnations. The stories related to them are many. They shed light on Avatara pantheon of Vishnu.

Indian tradition considers the works known as Akhyana, Itihasa, Purana, etc. as a part of her mythology. Akhyana means communication of previous events, tale, story, legend. The word Itihasa can be explained as iti-ha-asa which means 'so indeed it was.' Pura means before, hense, Purana means material belonging to ancient, old, traditional heritage.

Vishnu finds place in all the itihasas, puranas and akhyanas of India. It forms the base of art, culture and literature of the country. Incarnations of Vishnu form the nucleus of Bhagvata Bhakti movement of India. Here is a brief survey of these traditions which sprang around Vishnu and his incarnations.

M.L. Varadpande

1

VISHNU

The Universe moves through constant and perpetual cycles of creation, prerervation and destruction. All pervader, divinity Vishnu basically relates himself to the function of preservation of life and matter. Displaying Sattva quality he symbolizes life that he pervades. He establishes the rule of dharma, moral order, through his several incarnation. In this sense he is one and many.

Bhagavata Purana says : 'Just as from an inexhaustible lake thousands of streams flow on all sides, so also from Remover-of-Sorrow (Hari), sum of all reality, come forth countless incarnations. The seers, the low givers, the gods, the human race, the lords of progeny, all are parts of Him.'

From making small beginning in the Rig Veda, he gradually achieved the status of Supreme God in the Vedic period itself. He increased his influence by merging in him several divinities and their cults. His mythology grew by incorporating great Indian epics, Ramayana and Mahabharata, Purana works in part or full which speak of him and mostly of his incarnations.

In the Rig Veda 'he is celebrated in not more than five whole hymns and in part of another.' His name in this Veda occurs only about hundred times. According to some scholars he had imbibed the traits of solar divinity. Vishnu is wide-going and wide striding. Vishnu takes three steps traversing the earth or terrestrial spaces. According to one interpretation it indicates Sun's course, his rise, culmination and setting.

Macdonell in his Vedic Mythology says : 'He thrice traversed the earthly spaces for man in distress, he traversed the earth to bestow it on man for a dwelling, he traversed the earthly spaces for wide-stepping existence, with Indra he took wide strides and stretched out the worlds for our existence.' (p. 39)

Vishnu is a close friend of Indra, the warrior hero of the Vedas, Indra killed demon Vritra in the company with Vishnu. 'Vishnu and Indra together triumphed over the Dasa, destroyed Sambara's 99 castles and conquered the hosts of Varcin. Indra drank the Soma pressed by Vishnu in three cups. Vishnu also cooks for Indra 100 buffaloes and a brew of milk. Along with Mitra, Varuna and the Maruts Vishnu celebrates Indra with songs.' (Macdonell p. 39-40)

In the Vedic literature, Macdonell points out, Vishnu is described as beneficent, innocuous and bountiful, liberal and generous deliverer and alone sustains the threefold (world), heaven and earth and all beings.

In the Rig Veda Vishnu is called Gopa, the herdsman (Vishnurgopa RV 1.22.18). His highest abode, says Rig Veda, is full of many horned swiftly moving cows. Later Baudhayana Dharma-Sutra calls him Govinda the cow keeper and Damodara. Damodara means one with the cord around one's belly. It is a custom among herdsmen to tie a rope around around their waist. These associations of Vishnu later connected Krishna the cowherd with him. The Vedic legend of Vishnu being a cowherd lingered on in racial memory. For, poet Kalidasa in his Meghaduta compares dark cloud sporting a rainbow over it's body with dark-hued Vishnu in Gopa dress wearing a headgear of colourful peacock feathers.

In the Vedic literature Vishnu is equated with Yajna, the fire sacrifice. He is referred to with names such as Yajna, Yajnapurusha, Yajnavahana, etc. D.C. Sirkar says that according to Aiteraya Brahmana Vishnu averts the evil consequences of the defects in sacrifice. Sirkar further states that Vishnu had already became the greatest of god in later Vedic period. (The Cultural Heritage of India, Vol. IV, p. 110.

In the Rig Veda (Vll.100.5-6) Vishnu is addressed as Shipivishta, the term which is interpreted in different ways. According to one interpretation it may mean 'clothed with rays of light' and bald according to some scholars. However, R.N.Dandekar relates the word Shipi to Shepa meaning male phallus. Alain Danielou in his Hindu Polytheism writes : 'Louis Renou (L' Inde classique, p. 323) considers the origin of the name Vishnu as obscure and possibly non-Aryan. He mentions among the etymologies suggested by different scholars vi + sanu, 'crossing the nights' and vis,'active' and mentions the epithet sipi-vista, 'realised through the penis', indicating a possible phallic origin.' (p. 149) However the mythology do not support this interpretation.

Number of deities and their cults got assimilated in the Vedic religion of Vishnu. Narayana is one among them. He is not mentioned in the Vedas and for the first time reference is made to him in the Shatapatha Brahmana as a 'deity of considerable eminence.' He was further described as performer of Pancharatra-satra, ritual sacrifice spread over five days. In course of time Vasudeva—Krishna too was recognised as an incarnation of Vishnu. D.C. Sirkar writes : 'The earliest evidence in favour of the identification of Narayana with Vishnu probably to be traced in the Baudhayana Dharma-Sutra (about the fifth century B.C.). The Taittiriya Aranyaka (X.II) contains the passage. Narayanaya vidmahe Vasudevaya dhimahi, tan no Vishnuh pracodayat, in which Narayana, Vasudeva and Vishnu are regarded as one and the same deity. Here Narayana is aslo called Hari and the 'Eternal Deity', the Supreme, and Lord. But this part of Taittiriya Aranyaka is a later addition and appears to be considerably later than Baudhayana Dharma-Sutra. Several passages of Mahabharata support the identification of Vasudeva, Vishnu and Narayana as found in above passage.' (Cultural Heritage of India, Vol. IV, p. 119).

Vishnu usurped his own and of other's myths in Vedic literature to expand his sphere of influence. The story of his three strides and dwarf form by which he gained the whole earth from Asuras became the kernel of the myth of his Vamana incarnation. In the Taittiriya Samhita there *is a* story of a cosmogonic boar which raised the earth from primeval waters. This boar is described as a form of Prajapati. In the post-Vedic mythology this story is appended to Vishnu while speaking about his boar incarnation. The story of fish in Shatapatha Brahmana about saving Manu from great deluge is elaborated in the Mahabharata where this benevolent fish is described as a form of Prajapati. But in the Puranas this myth became central to Matsya incarnation of Vishnu.

Macdonell tells that in the Shatapatha Brahmana it is said that 'Prajapati about to create offspring becomes a tortoise moving in the primeval waters. In the Puranas this tortoise is an incarnation of Vishnu who assumes this form to recover various objects lost in the deluge.'

In the Vishnu Purana it is said that we bow before that Supreme Lord 'whom Yajnikas address as Yajnapurusha, Satvatas as Vasudeva and Vedantins as Vishnu.' (Panchama Ansha, 17th/Adyaya).'

He is called as Mayapati and assumer of forms such as Matsya, Kurma, Varaha, Hayagriva and Nrusimha.

Maya is considered as Vishnu's power of illusion, hence he is called Mayapati. She is identified in Samkhya with Prakriti and in that system as well as Vedanta, regarded as a source of Universe. Nobody can transcent the influence of Maya which is considered as inscrutable power of the Lord. It is maya who makes us think unreal as real. Creates the vision of deception and illusion. Only those who take refuse in Him escapes from the sphere of Maya.

P.K. Agrawala in his Goddesses in Ancient India states that basically in the Vedic literature, Maya appears to have been the prominent female deity of Asuras which means occult or mysterious power personified. She was not the deity of Aryan fold. But later Maya got associated with Vishnu as his power of illusion and hence he came to be known as Mayapati there are number of myths narrating the significance and scope of Vishnu's Maya.

In the Vaishnava mythology Maya is referred to as Vaishnavi Mahamaya or Yogamaya. In the Vishnu Purana (Panchama Ansha, Adhyaya 1) it is said that Vaishnvi Mahamaya assumed different names and forms such as those of Arya, Durga, Vedagarbha, Ambika, Bhadra, Bhadrakali, Kshemada, etc. The tribal or Asura origin of the goddess can be underlined by the fact that devotees were enjoined to offer her oblation of liquor and flesh.

In the Durga Saptashati (5th chapter, verses 7 and 16) it is said that among many other appelations goddess Durga is known as Vishnu Maya.

According to some scholars the worship of goddess Kamakhya of Kamarupa was initially supported by Vaishnavas. In his book Mother goddess Kamakhya Dr. Banikanta Kakati writes : 'Durga with her varied names had already established herself as a mighty goddess in the Puranic pantheon. In the Harivamsha she is called Narayanpriya (beloved of Narayana) and Vasudevabhagini (sister of Vasudeva) These epithets shew her early association with Vishnu and Vaishnavite cult. Commenting on this passage of Harivamsha Muir says: The object of this passage seems to be to take Durga and her worship under the patronage and protection of Vishnu.' (J. Muir Original Sanskrit Texts: Vol. IV, (1863) page 370). This will explain why the worship of Kamakhya was encouraged and patronised by Vishnu.' (p. 17)

Later Durga and Kamakhya both came under the influence of Shaivite cults and mythologically became closer to Shiva.

Number of folk and tribal deities got assimilated in the cult of Vishnu and attained the status of being his incarnation. Some scholars believe that originally Jagannatha of Puri was a tribal deity who was later recognised as Vishnu-Krishna. Suvira Jaiswal in her thesis Origin and Development opines that even Vasudeva and Balarama had an unmistakable tribal background. She further states that it is difficult to determine whether Narayana was an Aryan or non-Aryan. About Dattatreya who is recognised in some Puranas as an incarnation of Vishnu she feels that he, popular in Maharashtra, may have been a god of some local semi-civilised tribe which was Brahmanised through Vaisnivism.

Generally speaking ten incarnations of Vishnu are universally accepted. A Pallava inscription of the later half of the seventh century A.D. enumerates ten incarnations of Vishnu as follows : Fish, Tortoise, Boar, Man-lion, Rama (Parashu—), Rama (Dasharathi), Rama (Bala—), Buddha and Kalki. Jayadeva states that all these incarnations are of Krishna, yet another form of Vishnu.

However, to this list many names were added by different Puranans, particularly by Bhagavata Purana. The Bhagavata adds to this list the names of four Brahmins—Sanak, Sanandana, Sanatana and Sanat Kumar—, Devarshi Narad who propagated Satvata Tantra, Nara-Narayana, Kapil propagator of Samkhya philosophy, Dattatreya, Yajna, Rishabadeva son of king Nabhi, King Pruthu, Vyas author of Mahabharata.

Vishnudharmottara Purana speaks of Padmanabha, Mohini, Vishvarupa, Hansa, Hayagriva and Valmiki as incarnations of Vishnu. Vayu and Matsya purana includes the name of king Mandhata in the list.

Interestingly the names of Buddha founder of Buddhism and Jain Tirthankara Rishabhadeva too are included in the lists of some Puranas. Probably this was an effort to bring Buddhism and Jainism in Vaishnava fold.

1. Vishnu-18th Century, Gilt Copper, Bharat Kala Bhavan, Varanasi.

2. Sheshashayi Vishnu, Dashavtar Temple: Deogarh Lalitpur Distt. U.P. 500-525 AD. Red Sandstone.

3. Vishnu on Garuda Inscribed 10th Century Buff Sandstone, Allahabad Museum.

4. Vishnu Seshashayi, 10th Century, Sandstone, Mathura Museum.

5. Vishnu- Kalki Incarnation, early 10th Century; Kashmiara Style, Brass. J.K. Deosar S.P.S. Museum, Srinagar.

6. Vishnu, Parashuram Incarnation, 17th Century, Chamba, H.P., Bhuri Sinsh Museum, Chamba.

7. Vishnu Yogasana, 10th Century, Dahala Style, Sandstone M.P.

8.14th Armed Vishnu Astride Garuda, Vishnu 14th Century; Black Sandstone Rajputana Museum, Ajmer.

9. Lakshmi- Narayana on Garuda, 12th Century, Bronze.

10. Lakshmi- Narayan, 17th Century, Granite, Tanjore Art Gallery, Tanjore.

11. Lakshmi Narayan, Sandstone, 8th-14th Century, A.D. Khajurao, M.P.

12. Matsya Avatara, 11th Century, Plum Colured, Sandstone.

13. Kurma/Kacchapa Avatara, Side View, 11th Century, Plum Coloured Sandstone.

14. Varaha View from East 10-11th Century East, of Kari Talai in ruins of Vishnu-Varaha Temple, Red Sandstone.

15. Varah Alitting earth, early 5th Century, Buff Sandstone. Cave 5 Udayagiri, Vidisha Distt. M.P.

16. Narsimha, 12th Century, Kashmira Style, Grey Lime Stone, SPS Museum, Srinagar.

17. Vaman Tri Vikrama Mysore, Badami, Bijapur Distt., Cave 2, Mukhamandapa, West Wall. Last Quarter of 6th Century Sandstone.

18. Vamana, Grey Sandstone, 11th Century Khajurao, M.P. Allahabad Museum.

19. Ramayana Scene, Hanuman Adoring Rama. Mid 5th Century, Buff Sandstone, Nachna Kuthara, Patna Distt.

20. Balaram with Revati, Parshvanath Temple, Khajuraho.

21. Krishna Venu Gopal, AD 1196, Soap Stone, Amritpur, Mysore.

22. Buddha Seated in Bhumi Sparsha Mudra, 9th Century, Bronze, Nalanda, Patna Distt. Nalanda Museum.

Vishnu is conceived as one having certain attributes like conch, discus, mace, lotus flower, bow, arrows and quiver, brilliant Jem, garland of forest flowers, etc. His images are made having some or more of these attributes. Vishnu purana has explained symbolic meaning of these attributes like many other similar scriptures.

Sudarshan is a fearful weapon which he uses to kill the demons or deadly enemies. There are number of Puranic legend about its origin. According to one Shiva created it at the time of his expedition against demon Tripura. Vishnu performed penance to obtain it from Mahadeva. According to Mahabharata Agni, god of fire, obtained it from Varuna, Lord of Waters, and gave it to Krishna when mighty king Jarasandha attacked Mathura. Krishna used it frequently. It is said that once Ashvatthama, son of Dronacharya, asked for it in exchange of deadly Bramasiras Astra. Krishna showing his finger carry it to him said that he may take it. Ashvatthama prided himself for his immense strength but he could not remove Sudarshana from Krishna's finger though he applied all his strength.

In the nineth canto of Bhagavata Purana there is a story of Vishnu's devotee king Ambarisha's clash with wrathful sage Durvasa. Durvasa created a female demoness, Kritya, to kill Ambarisha. Vishnu used his Sudershana to destroy her. After her destruction Sudershana moved against Durvasa. Frightened sage went to Vaikuntha, abode of Vishnu, to get rid of it. Vishnu asked him to ask for the pardon of the king Ambarisha.

In this context there are several verses sung by Ambarisha in praise of Sudarshana.

Sudarshana is described as Kala Chakra in Vamana Purana. It had twelve spokes representing twelve months presided over by twelve deities. The central nave represented six seasons. Vishnu Purana says that Chakra symbolizes extremely agile mind which can defeat even wind in its speed. Some consider it to be luminious disk of sun itself.

The concept and symbol of Chakra has a great significance in the Buddhist religion. The launcing of the new religion by Buddha at Sarnatha is described as "Dharma Chakra Pravartana" or setting the wheel of law in motion". On early Buddhist stupas we find the scenes of Chakrapuja sculpted, quite frequently. Dharma Chakra on Buddhist mounments is suggestive of the presence of Buddha himself.

Vishnu's Chakra is there to vanquish external enemies of mankind referred into scriptures as Rakshasas, Asuras and such decoinim evil forces. Dharma Chakra is set into motion to eliminate internal enemies of human being such as lust, greed to help him achieve Nirvana that is cessation of sorrow. Each has its own function.

Though independant Chakra images alone can be found in most of the Vishnu temples, seperate shrines for Chakra in personified form are extremely rare. In Kanchipuram's Varadaraja temple complex, estern side of the temple tank, is located a temple of Chakra talvar (Sudarshana). Some of the older temples in South India like Srirangam and Tirumalai such shrines are found.

In the Balakanda of Ramayana the history of the bow of Vishnu is recorded. According to the epic Vishvakarma, the architect of gods, made two most powerful bows in the universe. One he gave to Shiva when he was waging war with demon Tripurasura and another he gave to Vishnu. To test who among the two, Vishnu and Shiva, was more powerful Brahma created strife among them. Due to that great fight ensued among them to establish who among them was more powerful. Just by making hum-kara sound Vishnu made Shiva and his bow ineffective, Rishis and Devatas declared Vishnu as greater god.

Then Rudra-Shiva gave his bow to Rajarshi Devarata of Videha and Vishnu gave his bow to Richikamuni of Bhrugu clan. From there the bow of Vishnu fell into the hands of Jamadagni, his son, and finally Parashurama possessed it.

At the time of Sita Swayamvara Dasharathi Rama broke the mighty bow of Shiva and won Sita's hand. Later Rama humiliated Parashurama by putting a twang on the mighty bow which Parashurama thought was impossible for any human being.

According to yet, another version describing the bow of Vishnu it is said that it's name was Saranga. Vishnu Purana states that it represents Indriya and Ahamkara. The Purana further states that, the numerous arrows of Vishnu are the senses, the fields of activity of intellect and the guiver is the storehouse of actions. (Danielou Polytheism Hindu p. 156).

The conch is yet another attribute of Vishnu. According to one popular verse, not found in Puranas, the conch was product of Samudra Manthana, churning of the ocean by gods and demons, to obtain Amrita, elixir of life. Vishnu Purana says that conch and bow Vishnu carries represents Tamas and Rajas Ahamkara caused by Bhutas and Indriyas.

The name of Vishnu-Krishna's conch is Panchajanya, representing five elements - Prithvi, Tej, Vayu, Akasha, Jala.

According to a legend in Devi Bhagavata the conches were product of bones of demon Shankhachuda killed by Shiva. Vishnu blessed him that conches and leaves of plant form of his wife's hair, Tulasi, will be part of his worship.

In the Bhagavata Purana it is said that there lived a demon named Panchajana in the ocean in the form of *a* conch. He kidnapped and killed the son of Sandipani, teacher of Krishna. Krishna killed him and brought the conch made out of his body with him.

Mahabharata says when Krishna blew his Panchajanya conch followed by blowing of their respective conches by the warriors from Pandava's side on the battle field of Kurukshetra, that tremedous sound reverberating through heaven and earth pierced the hearts of the sons of Dhritarashtra.

Vishnu hold mace in one of his four hands. It is a powerful weapon filling the hearts of enemies with fear. It, according to Vishnu Purana, represents the power of mind. Alain Danielou writes: 'The power of knowledge dazzles and intoxicates the mind hence it (the mace) is called the stupefire-of-the-mand—Kaumodaki. The power of knowledge is the essence of life (prana tattva) from which all physical and mental powers are derived. Nothing else can conquer time and itself become power of time. As such the mace is identified with the goddess Kali who is the power of time. The mace is Kali, power of time. It destroys all that apposes it. '(Hindy Polytheism, p. 157)

Lotus is very dear to Vishnu which he holds in one of his four hands. Lotus is symbol of purity and auspiciousness. Beautiful wife of Vishnu, Lakshmi, deity of wealth and prosperity is always depicted as one sitting on lotus flower. Hence she is called Padma or Padmaja. According to yet another legend, Brahma the Lord of Creations, sits on the flower bearing lotus plant that sprouts from the navel of Vishnu sleeping in the waters of Kshirasagara. Thus lotus in the hand of Vishnu symbolizes creation and sustainance of the universe.

Vishnu is a warrior deity having weapons such as bow and arrows. Vishnu's bow is known as Saranga. 'The bow is the destructive-notion-of-indivisual-existence (tamasa Ahamkara), the aspect that is associated with the disintegrating tendency and origin of the senses (Vishnu Purana-1.22.70). The numerous arrows of Vishnu are the senses, the fields of activity of the intellect. (Vishnu Purana 1.22.73)' (Hindu Polytheism, p. 156)

Shine brightly on the chest of Vishnu is a jem known as Kaustubha. According to a popular verse enlisting 14 objectes that arose from the Samudra Manthan, churning of the ocean, one was Kaustubha. Ramayana and the

Mahabharata too speaks of Kaustubha as treasure of the ocean. Vishnu Purana says: 'The soul of the world, unsoiled, subtle, pure is jewel.'

Vaijayantimala which Vishnu wears around his neck is Pancharupa that is made of five kinds of precious jems - Mukta, Manikya, Marakat, Indranil and Hirak. It is collective form of Panchatanmatras and Panchabhutas. Vishnu Purana says : Achyuta holds a sparkling Nandak sword which is nothing but 'vidyamaya jnan' covered with the sheath of 'avidyamaya kosha'.

Delinating the inner meaning of the attributes of Vishnu thus, the Vishnu Purana says: 'Likewise we find Purusha, Pradhan, Buddhi, Ahamkar, Panchabhuta, Mana, Indriya, Vidya and Avidya remain subservient to Vishnu in the forms of weapons.

Vishnu had a chariot drawn by four horses which according to Mahabharata 'moves at will like swift mind'. Vishnu wears ornaments such as crown (kirita), ear ornaments known as makara (sea monster shaped) and armlets. The yellow garment he wears is called Pitambara. His complexion is lustrous blue-black, like a sky or cloud in rainy season. Garuda is his fast moving bird vehical and he sleeps on the coils of serpent.

An interesting concept of Ayudha Purushas was mooted by playwright Bhasa, ascribed to 4th-5th century B.C. (and to 3rd century A.D. by some) in his play Duta Vakyam based on the episode in the Mahabharata related to a peace mission of Krishna to Kaurava court, the last effort by him to avert the war.

It seems that Bhasa belonged to the cult of Vishnu as Vasudeva-Krishna. In opening songs of his plays he has betrayed the knowledge of Vishnu and his names and incarnations such as Narayana, Vasudeva, Sridhara, Keshava, Damodara, Varaha, Vamana, Narasimha, Rama and Krishna. He also wrote plays based on legends of Rama and Krishna.

Ayudha Purusha means weapons of Vishnu or Krishna in human form. In the Bhasa's play Dutavakyam we see Krishna trying to broker peace between Kauravas and Pandavas. Bent upon declaring war prince Duryodhana tries to arrest him. Angry Krishna manefest in his frightening Vishvarupa form and invite his weapons to appear. The weapons appear one by one in human form. They include disk Sudarshana, bow Saranga, Kaumodaki mace Panchajanya conch, Nandak sword and bird vehicle Garuda. Their detail physical description is given in the play.

Sculptors translated the concept of Ayudha Purushas and made them into representative sculptures. In the Dashavatara temple at Deogarh (Jhansi) in Central India ascribed to 6th-7th century A.D. there is a large image of Vishnu sleeping on the coils of serpent Shesha. Lakshmi is seen massaging his feet. Beneath this magnificient sculptre there is a row of Ayudha Purushas. Generally one or many Ayudha Purushas are sculpted at the feet of some Vishnu images.

Lakshmi, goddess of wealth, beauty, fertility, also known by several other names such as Kamala, Sri, emerged as consort of Vishnu.

Initially Sri and Lakshmi were two seperate and distinct entities as is evident from Vedic literature. P.K. Agrawala says that identification of these two deities is arrived only in the Srisukta, a hymn glorifying Sri, and appended as a Khila to the fifth book of the Rig Veda. In this hymn the cult of Sri (Lakshmi) appears to have found its popular sanction. He concludes that at this period of time Sri and Lakshmi were identified as two names of the single divinity.

In the Yajurveda (31.22) Sri and Lakshmi are described as wives of Spreme Being or Cosmic Purusha. In later literature Purusha is identified with Vishnu.

A view has been expressed by Gerda Hartmann in her study on the goddess Lakshmi regarding her as a pre-Aryan goddess of fertility. According to her the several phenomena and functions related to Sri—Lakshmi's character, cult, mythology and iconography how a variety of traits characteristic of deities concerned with fertility and prosperity in general. (Goddesses in Ancient India, p. 92).

Sri or Siri alias Lakshmi or Lakkhi had a popular following as is evident from Buddhist Siri Kalakanni Jataka. On the railing of Bharhut Stupa we find sculptural representation of Sirimao Devata. Devangana Desai writes: 'Her complete acceptance by Buddhist is evidenced in numerous images of her at Sanchi, Bharhut, Bodha Gaya, Pitalkhora, etc. The most common form of representation is Sri flanked by two elephants (nagas) who keep her ardra (moist) by pouring water on her. This symbolizes 'the fertilization being representing, or connected with the earth or the fields by rain clouds; clouds were often represented by elephants, the word naga having both meanings. At Bharhut the fertile Sri stands on a lotus growing out of bhadra-ghata or auspicious pot, holds a lotus in her left hand and touches with her right hand her own breast which is gesture symbolizing abundance and bounty. '(Erotic Sculpture of India, p. 19)

Lakshmi is generally shown standing or sitting on lotus flower flanked by two elephants pouring water on her or holding lotus flowers in their trunks raised upwards.

Most popular legend about the emergence of Lakshmi is found in the Mahabharata. It says when gods and demons churned ocean to obtain elixir of life, Amrita, among the things that emerged one was Sri. Bhagavata Purana has given elaborate account of the myth.

Bhagavata Purana says that when beautiful Lakshmi emerged from the ocean with lotus flower in her hand the Diggajas (four elephants representing four quarters) bathed her by pourping water from auspicious pots. She then chose Bhagavan Vishnu as her consort.

We start getting the Lakshmi images along with Vishnu since Gupta period. The best example is found at Deogarh where Lakshmi is shown at the feet of Vishnu reclinig on the coils of serpent Shesha massaging his feet. Such image of Vishnu is known by the name of Anantashayanam, Sheshashayin, Jalashayin, etc. N.P. Joshi in his Bharatiya Murtishastra says that in post Gupta period the tradition of showing gods with their consorts flourished. Sometimes they are shown as sitting together on Garuda, their bird vehicle.

It is believed that Lakshmi takes incarnation along with her Lord on the earth. On the number of Narasimha images Lakshmi is shown sitting on his lap. In Vishnu's Rama incarnation Lakshmi was Sita. In his Krishna incarnation Lakshmi became Rukmini. According to Oria tradition G.N. Mohapatra writes: 'Jagannatha cult is basically a development of Lakshmi-Narayana worship which was very popular in Orissa long ago. That was the time of Jayadeva when Vaishnava (Ganga kings were ruling over Orissa and Jagannatha was accepted as Vishnu Krishna and his Shakti to be conceived as Lakshmi -Radha. (Jagannatha in History and Religious Traditions of Orissa, p. 17)

In the Moksha Dharma Parva of the Shanti Parva of Mahabharta Lakshmi tells Indra that she emerged from lotus which was fully bloomed by the heat of sun— rays and her names were Padma, Sri and Padmamalini also. She told him that initially she used to live among Daityas (demons) due to their excellent moral behaviour and clean habits. But gradually all kinds of corruption set in among them and she left them to stay with gods. Detail description of moral behaviour which Lakshmi likes is given in this chapter in the Mahabharata.

Brahmavaivarta Purana says that Lord Vishnu had three wives — Saraswati, Ganga and Lakshmi. Once

Saraswati became angry with Ganga for her efforts to be close to her Lord. Lakshmi tried to passify them both but angry Saraswati rubuked her also. They cursed each other and as a result Saraswati became river along with Ganga. Lakshmi too became a river named Padmavati and a auspicious plant named Tulasi.

Another version of Tulsi story is found again in the same Purana. A cowherd girl of Goloka named Tulsi was born on the earth as a daughter of King Dharmadwaja. She married demon king Shankhachuda who in his previous incarnation was a cowherd named Sudama. Tulsi was 'pativrata' that is extremely faithful to her husband. It was not possible for gods to destroy the demon Shankhachuda unless they breached the pativratya of Tulsi. Hence Vishnu one day assumed the form of Shankhachuda and made love to Tulsi defiling her. Tulsi wept profusely but by the blessings of Vishnu she became a river on the earth called Gandaki and also the most auspicious plant named Tulsi or Vrinda. Vishnu is delighted when worshipped with the leaves of Tulsi which is also known as Vrinda plant. Vishnu became Shaligram stone in river Gandaki.

There are certain interesting Puranic and folk tales highlighting relationship of Lakshmi and her consort Vishnu, some quite humorous. In Orissa, every.year in the luner month of Margashirsha Oriya women worship goddess Lakshmi on every Thursday. A scripture known as Mahalakshrai Purana is very popular in Orissa which narrates a very interesting story of Lakshmi and her husband Vishnu-Jagannatha.

On one thursday of Margashirsha Lakshmi went out of her abode, the magnificent Jagannatha temple at Puri, to receive worship from her female devotees. During her wandering she saw a very low caste woman, Sriya Chandaluni, living in a small village, worshipping Lakshmi with great devotion.

Lakshmi was immensely pleased to see her devotion. She entered her ramshakle hut, accepted her worship and even food cooked by her with great delight.

When Balabhadra, elder brother of Lord Jagannatha, came to know about Lakshmi's unacceptable behaviour of accepting the food prepared by a very low caste woman belonging to Chandala caste, he became furious and ordered his brother not to allow her entry into their abode.

To execute the order of his elder brother Lord Jagannatha himself along with the temple guards stood at the main gate of the temple, the Simha Dwara, to stop Lakshmi from entering their abode.

When Lakshmi returned to the temple after accepting worship from her house-wife devotees Lord Jagannatha stopped her at the entrace gate. When she asked the reason for his crude behaviour Lord told her that as she had become impure by accepting food made by Chandalini she can not enter the holy temple and defile it..

Lakshmi told her Lord that she was going away and soon he would reap the consequences of his actions.

In the night when two brothers were under the spell of sleep in the temple Lakshmi ordered her ferocious Vetala attendent to divest the temple of all its riches and everything it possessed by her grace.

Overnight the Lords became paupers, no descent cloths to wear, no food to eat, no water to drink. Compelled by excessive they were required to roam in the streets like beggers. Nobody would offer them food. If someone dared all the goods in his house would disappear due to the wrath of Lakshmi.

Wandering around they reached the sea-shore. There they saw a magnificent golden palace. They were informed that it was owned by a Chandala but if they would go there food would be served to them out of pity.

Caste conscious Balabhadra asked the servants of the palace who received them to provide them with raw material for cooking their meals as they would not eat the food made by low caste Chandalas. The material was provided but they failed to cook it as fire would not burn due to magic powers of Lakshmi.

Ultimately the Lords decided to take the food cooked in the Chandala household due to the pangs of excessive hunger from which they were suffering from days at a stretch. When the food was served to them it seemed to be very much familiar. It was a food which Lakshmi used to give them in the temple. Baladeva realised his mistake and both of them profusely apologised for insulting Lakshmi, the all powerful goddess of wealth and prosperity. She returned with them to temple pardoning them.

Another legend about Lakshmi - Jagannatha is equally interesting. During Ratha Yatra Jagannatha takes Subhadra, his sister, alongwith him ignoring Lakshmi. On his return to the temple after Ratha Yatra angry Lakshmi, represented by her Pandas, refused the Lord to enter the temple and there ensues a quarrel.

Mohapatra Informs that 'Jagannatha himself is also known as the form of Nilamadhava who was being worshipped with Lakshmi in Niladri since long before. Before the arrival of Jayadeva the Madhava cult was popular in Orissa. Most of the Madhava images were worshipped with Lakshmi. From that angle of vision Nilamadhava-Jagannatha of Puri carrying more importance attracted the mind of poet to come over there as the foremost devotee of Madhava. But as a Vaishnava follower of Nimbarka, etc, he tried to assimilate Radha with Lakshmi and generalised Krishna as Madhava Jagadisha.

Radha in the Gita Gtovinda is referred to by different names of Lakshmi. However, it is interesting to note that there is no shrine dedicated to Radha in the premises of Jagannatha temple but there is one dedicated to Lakshmi.

By the side of Jagannatha in Puri temple there is a metal image of Lakshmi.

Lakshmi is worshipped on many occasions and number of Vratas (vows) are performed in her honour but the most important worship to her is offered on the day of Lakshmi Pujan, Kartika Amavasya, which is the main part of festival of lights or Dipavali.

There is no independent cult of Lakshmi but the Sri Vaishnavas of South India which emerged around eleventh century A.D. gives utmost importance to Sri-Lakshmi as a consort of Vishnu. She is recognised as a Lotus Lady and inseperable breast-jewel of Vishnu. The devotees pray her with following verse. They say: 'I bow down before Sri, the mother of all, who resides on the lotus, has eyes of blossoming lotuses and who reclines on the heart of Vishnu.' Sri is considered as one who mediates between a devotee and Vishnu, her lord.

Due to ways Lakshmi serves her Lord by remaining at her feet she was traditionally considered as an icon of Indian womanhood.

There are number of legends regarding Vishnu (and his incarnations) rushing to the help of his devotees at the difficult times. In fact this is one of the declared aims of taking incarnation according to Bhagavad Gita. In this context two stories are very popular - one is of King Ambarisha and another of deliverance of an elephant (Gajendra Moksha). Both these stories are found in the Bhagavata Purana.

King Ambarisha was son of Nabhaga. He was great devotee of Yajnapurusha Vishnu and his incarnation Krishna. He performed numerous Yajnas in the dry country named Dhanva on the bank of river Saraswati. Pleased by his devotion Srihari deputed his terrible weapon, Sudarshana Chakra.

His wife too was devotee of Hari. Once both of them decided to observe Ekadashi Vrata for one full year. At the close of Vrata in the month of Kartik observed fast for three days.

Then after taking sacred bath in river Kalindi he worshipped Hari in the Madhuvana with appropriate rituals. Then he started preparations for Parana or concluding function of the Vrata.

As luck would have it ever-angry sage Durvasa arrived on the scene. Most humbly Ambarisha requested him to take meals at his place. Accepting his invitation Durvasa went to take bath in river Yamuna. But he did not return in time. Dwadashi was about to start and it was imperative for Ambarisha to break fast before that. He consulted Brahmins who told him that he can break fast by drinking water. Ambarisha did exactly that as was required according to the rules prescribed by Vrata.

When Durvasa returned and found that Ambarisha had broken the fast without feeding him first he became extremely angry. He plucked a bunch of hair from his Jata on the head and banged on the earth. Instantly a female evil spirit, Kritya, emerged out of it. With all ferocity she attacked king Ambarisha. But the king did not budge from his place.

Before Kritya could reach the king, Sudarshana Chakra, which was deputed to protect him by Vishnu, burnt her within a second. Then angry Chakra went after Durvasa with all fury. Durvasa ran for his life but Chakra did not stop following him. Whenever he went Chakra went after him. Ultimately he went to Lord Brahma. But Brahma told him that he had no powers to hold back Vishnu's Chakra. From there Durvasha rushed to Lord Shiva but he too pleaded his inability to control Chakra. Thinking that Lord Vishnu would stop his formidable weapon from persuing him he surrended before him. But Vishnu refused to oblige the sage. He asked him to fall at the feet of Ambarisha himself. When Durvasa did that Chakra spared him.

This is how the Lord protects his devotees.

Another story, famously known as Gajendra Moksha, too is from Bhagavata Purana. There was a great mountain named Trikuta which had three peaks of gold, silver and iron. Covered with dense forest it was habited by sem-divine beings like Siddha, Charana, Gandharva, Naga, Kinner and apsara. It was infested with terrible beasts like lion and tiger.

In the forest there was a garden of Lord Varuna whose name was Rituman. One day a herd of elephants led by their leader Gajendra came to drink water in the tank. Seeing its expanse the elephants entered into it. But a powerful crocodile got hold of the leg of Gajendra. He offered prayers to Lord Vishnu and astride his bird-vehicle Garud he rushed to save Gajendra. When he saw Hari in the sky he plucked a lotus flower with his trunk and lifted it up in his direction.

Lord jumped from the back of Garud and dragged both Gajendra and Nakra out of water. In his previous life the Nakra was a great Gandharva named Huhu and the Gajendra was none else but king Indradyumna. They assumed their own forms and by the grace of Lord Vishnu went to Vaikuntha.

In numerous incarnations of Vishnu what we see is his 'lila'. Lila means play, sport, diversion, amusement. In the context of Indian theology the term acquires specific meaning. Lila is sportful activity of the god and his incarnations, divine acts in space and time.

Norvin Hein in his Miracle Plays of Mathura says: 'A major tradition of Hindu thought describes as 'sports' the whole of divine acts in space and time. Confronted with the problem of how the Supreme Being, while oximatically perfect and self-sufficient, could yet have had a reason to produce the cosmos. Hindu thinkers have long taught that creation, preservation and dissolution of worlds spring from no lack of need on the part of God, but are the manifestations of his spontaneous joyful disinterested creativity - are his sports. Not only Vishnu's creation of cosmos is viewed as lila, but his actions within the cosmos when he enters his creation in the form of various incarnations (p. 70).

Goswami Tulsidas in the Uttarkanda of his Ramcharitmanas says that an actor dances by wearing number of costumes and shows expressions according to his roles but he is different from the character he is portraying. Such is the lila of Raghupati.

In the Bhagavata Purana Krishna and Balarama are likened to two actors in the same sence.

Garud is the bird-vehicle of Vishnu. The story of Garud is quite elaborately narrated in the Adiparva of the epic Mahabharata. He was second son of Maharshi Kashyapa and his wife Vinita. In the Vedic literature a bird called Shyena is mentioned who brought Soma on the earth. Hence, Soma came to be known as Shyenabhrita. Some scholars think that Garud is a Pauranic form of vedic Shyena. As Shegna brought Soraa on the earth from heaven Garud brought Imrita on the earth from heaven.

There arose some dispute between two co-wives of Kashyapa, Vinita and Kadru, the mother of serpents. Kadru won and Vinita was made to become her slave.

Kadru told Garud that if he will bring Amrita from heaven for her she will free his mother from the bond of slavery. Garud went to heaven, fought with gods guarding Amrita on earth.

When he was flying through the sky with Amrita Bhagvan Vishnu saw him. Vishnu noticed that though he was carrying the pot of Amrita he did not swollow even a single drop of elixir of life which could have made him immortal. Pleased by his integrity Vishnu requested him to remain stationed on his flag when he was riding his chariot. He became the bird vehicle of the Lord also.

Once Indra, king of gods, pleased with a serpent Sumukha made him immortal. Garud who considered all the snakes on the earth as his natural prey became angry. He started boasting that he is all powerful, more powerful than Vishnu himself, as he carries him with ease. *To* shatter his pride and ego, Vishnu just placed his arm on him. Garud became breathless and started panting. He surrendered to Vishnu who placed the snake sumukha on his chest.

He killed number of demons. According to Valmiki Ramayana when Vishnu was hurt fighting demon Malyavan he moved him away from the battlefield. Once, as ordered by Vishnu he freed king Uparichara Vasu from his captivity in Patala loka.

N.P. Joshi writes in his Bharatiya Murtishastra that images of Vishnu astride Garud are rare in Kushana period. In the Mathura Museum there is one such tiny images which can be ascribed to post Kushana period. Till then Garud was sculpted as a bird. Gradually he evolved into an animal having human body with wings and face of a bird. In the post Gupta period the images of Vishnu and Lakshmi astride Garuda were also made at Khajuraho we see eight armed Vishnu astride Sarudin in semi-human form. In number of Vishnu temples Garud is shown facing his image standing near sanctum with folded hands.

Once upon a time there lived two friends, one carpentar and other weaver, in a certain city. Since childhood they intensely loved each other and used to spend their time together. Once in their city a grand festival of local deity took place. To attend it dancers, singers, wandering entertainers arrived in the city along- with hundreds of people from different countries. Both the friends mingling in their crowd started moving around enjoying the festival.

Suddenly they saw a beautiful princess adorned with jewellery protected by old Brahmins and eunuch attached to her harem astride an elephant moving towards the temple of deity to worship it.

Struck by her beauty the young weaver, struck by the arrow of Cupid, lost his consciousness and fell down on the earth as if stung by poison or suffering from the ill effect of evil planet.

Seeing his condition the carpenter became worried. With the help of some people around he lifted him up and carried him to his house. After some time being treated by a physician and magical spells of witch doctors he came to his senses.

Worried carpenter asked his friend as to what was the cause of his becoming unconscious?

Weaver said to his friend that if he wanted to do him a favour he should prepare a funeral pyre and let him burn on it.

His friends words brought tears to the eyes of carpenter. There must have been some reason for his saying so, he thought. 'There is no problem on the earth which can not be solved, he said, assuring him of all help.

After much persuation weaver said that the sight of that beautiful girl astride the elephant who had come to attend the festival of local deity was the cause of his distress. When would he be able to hold that beautiful girl who had full and firm bosoms like temples of an elephant'smeared with wet safforn paste, in his arms and make love to her, he lamented. Her red lips like Bimba fruits, bosoms like pitchers, pride of youth, deep navel naturally curly hair, slim waist and bright cheeks made his heart burn, he told his friend.

Carpenter started laughing after hearing the love-lorn lament of his friend. If this is the case, he told him, he should prepare himself to make love to her that very night.

Did he know that except for the gentle breeze of wind nothing is allowed to enter her royal chamber? The weaver lad asked.

The carpenter told him that he would make for him a replica of Garuda bird which could fly in the air with the turing of mechanical devise fitted inside its body. Along with it he would make two artificial wooden hands and things like shankha, chakra, gada, padma, kirit and kaustubha, all symbols of Vishnu, for him to wear. In the garb of Vishnu he should, astride the mechanical Garuda, enter the seventh story palace bed-room of the princess and pretending that he was Lord Vishnu Himself seduce her. The innocent inexperienced girl thinking you to be Vasudeva himself submit to your desire. Pleasing her with clever and glib talk make love to her using the techniques devised by Muni Vatsyayana.

Delighted by his friend's advise the weaver in the garb of Vishnu flew into the bed chamber of the princes in the night and told her that leaving behind loving wife Lakshmi alone in the ocean, their abode, he had come to make love to her.

Seeing Vishnu himself standing before her surprised princess told him that she was just an ordinary human being and he a divinity, how can they unite in love ?

Clever carpenter told her that what she said was indeed a fact. But she was none else but Radha, one of his wives who was born in the family of cowherds in the Dwapara yuga.The same beautiful Radha had incarnated in her form, hence he had come there.

Princess told him that if indeed such was the case he should approach her father who would gladly give her to him gladly.

Pretending anger the carpenter told her that what of talking to him ordinary human beings even can not see him in his divine form. Adopting the custom of Gandharva union she should immediately submit to his desire or he would not hesitate to inflict a curse on her family and burn them all along with her father.

After saying this, getting down from his Garuda vehicle, he held the hand of princess trembling with fright and bashfulness and took her to bed and enjoyed her till morning by using the love techniques formulated by Muni Vatsyayana.

In the morning the weaver departed fully satisfied. Now it became his daily routine to visit the princess and make love to her.

Seeing the marks of lovemaking including the male teeth marks on the lips of the princess the harem staff went into tizzy. They reported the matter to her father, the king.

Lamenting over the fact king thought that after all having a daughter was a root cause of trouble and worry for parents. River and women were the same in their behaviour. Banks of the river were like girl's maternal and paternal families. River by her floods and women by their faults destroy the family completely.

Angry parents visited the palace of their daughter and rebuked her severely for her behaviour. Banding her head with shame and fear the princess said that every night Lord Narayana himself visited her. If they had any doubt they should see it for themselves.

After seeing the weaver in the guise of Vishnu coming to their daughter's chamber in the night the parents of the princess, the king and the queen, got delighted.

The king thought that when Lord Narayana himself courted his daughter he could now fulfill his ambitious plan to defeat all the neighbouring kings and become the master of the entire earth.

With this in mind the king started coming in conflict with neighbouring kings. Angered by his behaviour all the neighbouring kings formed a alliance and attacked his territory with their armies. But he was not worried he asked his daughter to tell Bhagavan Narayana to kill his enemy forces. In a message which he asked his daughter to deliver king said that was it proper for enemy forces to invade his territory when Bhagvan Narayana himself was his son-in-law?

Listening to this message delivered to him by his beloved princess the weaver bragged about his divine prowess and told her that with his weapon, the Sudarshana Chakra, he would cut the enemy forces to pieces.

Meanwhile the enemy forces made tremendous advances in his territory. Ultimately only one fort was left with him. The king asked his daughter to acquaint Lord Narayana with the emergency situation and request him to act fast.

Compelled by the circumstances the weaver in the guise of Vishnu decided to appear before enemy forces. He thought that would probably frighten the enemy soldiers, away. He asked the princess to tell her father to assemble large army and in the morning coming out of the city attack the enemy forces. He would fly with them in the sky and provide them required support by participating in the war.

The weaver knew that his death was certain but he had no other alternative but to act.

Bhagavan Narayana, the real one, called his bird vehicle, Garuda and asked him if he knew that one weaver in his guise astride a wooden Garuda visited the princess every night and enjoyed her person ? Garuda affirmed the fact. Bhagavan told Garuda that tomorrow morning in the desperate mood of do or die the weaver would attack the enemy forces. He was sure to die hit by the arrows of main warriors in the enemy army. This would certainly be detrimental to our reputation as great deities. This would lead people to think that the warriors killed Vasudeva and his bird vehicle and people would stop worshipping us. Hence, he must win. He would enter the body of the weaver and Garuda the body of wooden bird. We would fight and defeat enemy forces.

Saying this Bhagavan Narayana entered the body of the weaver. Soon unable to face the onslought of weaver with Narayana in his body the enemy army ran away.

People watching the fight were surprised by seeing Vishnu himself supporting the king from above the sky. The carpenter descended from the sky and narrated the whole story to the people from the very beginning. However, the king pleased by his bravery gave his daughter to him in marriage. Carpenter lived happily thereafter enjoying the pleasures of senses with his beloved princess. (Panchatantra)

In the Bhagavata Purana there is a story of a Brahmin named Ajamila, a great sinner, who just call out the name of Narayana Vishnu, albeit inadvertly, at the time of his death and on that single pious act reaches the abode of Vishnu.

The Purana says that in the city of Kanyakubja there lived a Brahmin lad Ajamila of excellent character. One day as desired by his father he went to forest to fetch flowers, fruits, sacred Kusha grass and fire wood called Samidha require to ignate ritual fire.

There he saw a low caste Shudra enjoying the liquors like Madhu and Maireya in the company of a harlot whose eyes were lolling due to excessive drinking. He was trying to please her by singing, dancing and indulging in love sports. He was again and again embracing the harlot with joy.

The sight of Shudra and harlot enjoying their lives passionately very much affected the mind of Ajamila. He could not control his mind and procured a harlot for himself and squandered the wealth of his forethers to please her. So much so that he discarded his young and pious wife for her.

He had ten sons from the harlot. To maintain such a large family he started indulging in unlawful activities such as theft, dacoity and gambling.

The name of Ajamila's youngest son was Narayana whom he loved most. One day, when his time to die came near, three attendants of Yama, the god of death, arrived at his doorsteps. They were terrible to look at and wore frightening expression over their distorted faces. Afraid of them Ajamila shouted out the name 'Narayana' his youngest son beconing for help.

As soon as Ajamila said 'Narayana' the attendants of Narayana Vishnu appeared on the scene and they saved him from the clutches of attendands of God of Death.

Repentant Ajamila, the great sinner, went into a temple in Haridwar and prayed Narayana for his deliverance. One day he left his mortal body on the bank of river Ganga and attendants of Narayana took him to Vaikuntha, abode of Narayana Vishnu.

This story is narrated to show that even great sinners could achieve the punya-lokas merely by reciting the sacred name of Narayana.

Story of Dhruva, an ardent devotee of Bhagavan Vishnu, is very famous in the Vaishnava mythology. It finds mention in number of scriptures including Mahabharata as well as in Vishnu and Bhagavata Puranas. Due to his firm resolve and severe penance he had a vision of the Lord himself when he was just five years old. In the galaxy there is a very bright star which is named after him.

King Uttanapada, son of Swayambhuva Manu, had two wives, Suruchi aad Suniti. Suruchi and her son Uttama were his favourite but not so his other wife Suniti and her son Dhruva.

Bhagavata Purana says that one day King Uttanapada was lovingly showing affection to his son Uttama sitting on his lap. Dhruva too wanted to share his father's affection by sitting on his lap. But father did not welcome him. His step mother too rebuked him using harsh words.

Dejected by his father when Dhruva went to his mother with tears in his eyes she told him that none else but only Bhagavan Adhokshaja Vishnu could help him.

With firm resolve to see Vishnu child Dhruva left the city of his father. Taking pity on him divine sage Narada met him. He tried to persuade the child to return home but Dhruva was firm in his resolve. He told Narada that he wanted to gain such a place for himself which is the best in all the three worlds from which nobody would be able to dislodge him.

Narada advised him to the sacred forest of Madhuvana on the bank of river Yamuna and perform penance. Moved by his devotion Lord Vishnu himself appeared before him and gave him the place among the galaxy which became famous as Dhruva loka.

Avatara literally means descent of a deity from his abode in suitable form for certain purpose. Beginning of this concept is found in ancient Vedic literature. In the Taittiriya Samhita Prajapati, lord-of progenys is said to have taken the form of a boar to raise the earth from boundless waters.

Number of gods took Avataras, incarnations, but in Puranic and epical religion Avatara mainly means Avataras of Vishnu.

The rationale of incarnations of Vishnu is best explained in the verses seven and eight of the fourth chapter of the Bhagavad Gita. Krishna tells Arjuna.

यदा यदा हि धर्मस्य ग्लानिर्भवति भारत।
अभ्युत्थानमधर्मस्य तदात्मानं सृजाम्यहम॥ (7)

परित्रणाय साधूनां विनाशाय च दुष्कृताम्।
धर्मसंस्थापनार्थाय सम्भवामि युगे युगे॥ (8)

When ever Dharma suffers decline and Adharma is on acendency I take birth on the earth. Age after age, for the upliftment of the good and destruction of evil, as well as to establish the order of Dharma, I incarnate again and again.

The word Dharma has a very wide connotation in Indian context. It may be law, justice, virtue, morality, religious tenets, righteous way of life. Sadhu means virtious people

It is the duty of the Supreme Lord to see smooth functioning of the Dharma and people following it.

But time is never constant, it moves on. The order is disturbed, goodness is in danger, the earth starts suffering from the deeds of the evil ones. Peaceful slumber of the Supreme Lord reclining on the coils of Ananta is disturbed. He shakes off his peaceful state and appear on the earth to set everything right in this or that form. Such appearance is called Avatara.

Supreme Lord never incarnate himself on earth because he is formless, nirguna nirakar Brahma. It is always part, Ansha, of him that assumes form which is infested with all his powers. Hence the incarnations, according to Vishnu Purana, are called Anshavatar. His incarnation as Krishna was so powerful and carried his full potency, Puranas started calling him Purnavatar, Supreme Lord himself. Poet Jayadeva in his Gita Govinda went a step further and stated that it was Krishna who took ten incarnations, Krishna and Vishnu being one and the same.

Vishnu Purana says:

भवतो यत्परं तत्वं
तन्न जानाति कश्चन।
अवतारेषु यद्रूपं
तदर्चन्ति दिवौकसः ॥

Nobody knows your essence, gods worship forms which appear as your incarnations (1.4.17).

Incarnations of Hari are virtually innumerable. Bhagavat Purana states: 'Just as from an inexhaustible lake thousands of streams flow on all sides so also from Hari, sum of all reality, come forth countless incarnations.The seers, lowgivers, the gods, the human races, the lords of progeny, all are parts of him. (1.3.26-27).

These two quotations - one from Vishnu Purana and other from Bhagavata need some analysis.

Vedas and particularly Upanishadas tried to understand what is 'tatva', essential nature of Brahman. For common people this highly Philosophical treatises became more enigmatic than the Brahman himself. So for him the works like Itihasa, Purana, Katha, Akyayika which contained myths, stories, fables, fiction, tales, legends, fiction were easy to approach emotionally. Spiritual nature of Vishnu could be understood easily through myths, stories, etc. Hence people started allying themselves to this kind of literature more and more. Epics and Puranas were common people's way to understand higher spiritual concepts.

It is no wonder the Mahabharata said that Vedas or Vedic literature could be understood, explained with the help of works like Itihasa, Purana, etc. — Itihasapuranabhya vedam samupambruhaet.

Itihasa Puranas made wonders and brought Vedic religion closer to people. It took tales, myths, legends that contained in Vedic literature and gave them new look by suitably changing them or elaborating upon them. For instance in Vedic literature Shakuntala, Dushyanta and Bharata story gets cursory mention, Mahabharata, a Itihasa work, made it into full story and Puranas turned it into various versions.

The authors of Itihasas, Puranas, Mahakavyas being creative people invented their own myths, legends that were not there in Vedic literature or even if they were there they were in minuscule form. They took characters from Vedic literature and weaved stories around them. We find many Rishis and Munis of Vedic literature appearing in new garb in Epical and Puranic literature. Same is the case of number of Vedic deities. Life of myths of Vedic literature got enriched and prolonged through Itihasa and Purana works.

In the Chandogya Upanisheda there is one Devakiputra Krishna disciple of Ghora Angirasa. In the Ṛig Veda various Krishnas are mentioned. One among them was enemy of Indra.

Itihasas and Puranas created their own Krishna out of this. But the philosophy Ghora Angirasa taught to Devakiputra Krishna is reflected in Bhagvad Gita and hostilities between Indra and Krishna too carried out further by Puranas as seen from the myths like Govardhana Puja and Parijatapaharana episode.

Even if we agree that Itihasa and Purana created their own hero (Krishna) they did not forget to assimilate in his character his Vedic antecedents.

But this does not mean that the authors of the Itihasa and Purana works solely depended on Vedic literature. It assimilated in their fold local folk and tribal myths, legends in large number. Numerous gods, goddesses, characters which we do not remotely find in Vedic literature get mention in Itihasa Purana works. Not only myths and legend but historical facts too became the part of new works. Hence character like Krishna is half history half legend or history mixed with legends. His killings of demons miraculously in Vrindavan in his childhood by his divine powers may be part of local legend but Kamsa, ruler of Mathura, Jarasandha ruler of Magadha and entire Bharata war could be history.

So, here before us is a huge literature to analyse and find out the elusive truth. We can only make plausible guess and still feel at a loss to understand whole complex set of evidence.

Vishnu is a Vedic deity but incarnations such as Kurma and Matsya are not part of his lore in Vedic literature. Seeds of the story of Vamana incarnation is indeed part of Vishnu mythology but Puranas gave it new twist. We do not find Vasudeva-Krishna and Dasharathi Rama as a part of Vishnu lore of Vedic literature. It had no knowledge of Balarama, Parashurama or Kalki.

Composers of Itihasa and Puranas gave new lease of life to Vishnu by adding some Vedic legends, declaring some historical personalities like Parashurama, Dasharathi Rama,

Vasudeva-Krishna as related to him and inventing pure imaginary characters as a part of his lore as Kalki. Many prominent Vedic deities like Indra and Varuna lost their sheen with the passage of time but launching incarnation theory the Itihasas and Puranas revived the importance of Vedic Vishnu.

It is very difficult to say who did it and how it happened in the course of evolution of Vishnu though many theories came up to explain the phenomenon. But one fact is certain that not very significant Vedic deity, Vishnu, with the help on his incarnations became Supreme Deity of Itihasa and Purana works.

Concept of incarnation works both ways. When we say that Rama is incarnation of Vishnu we raise him to the status of Vedic deity, at the same time we increase the sphere of influence of the Vedic deity Vishnu and increase its popularity by allying him to Rama.

Bhagavata Purana went a step ahead. Incarnating deity need not incarnate as deity alone. He can be anybody – a seer, lawgiver, human being all are parts of him.

When we say all are parts of him, all animate and inanimate universe form his part. So god can incarnate as an animal, bird, beast, tree, mountain, river – virtually any thing and everything. God becomes universal and devotee can worship him in any form. Vishnu can be a stone in Gandaki river or Brahma a mountain.

However the first organised list of incarnations of Vishnu was given out by epic Mahabharata.

It is very interesting to note that the concept of incarnation, though in different form, is found in Buddhist literature. In the Buddhist Jatakas numerous incarnations of Bodhisatva along with their indivisual tales are recorded. However they seemed to be outcome of the concept of rebirth than incarnation because incarnation has specific purpose and it generally is destruction of evil. Rebirth is a result of Karma of individual self.

Numbers and names of incarnations of Vishnu differ from Purana to Purana. According to Valmiki Ramayana they were five by name Varaha, Krishna, Rama, Parashuram and Trivikrama.

In the Shanti Parva of Mahabharata ten incarnations of Vishnu are enumerated and they are Hamsa, Kurma, Matsya, Varaha, Narasimha, Vaman, Parashuram, Ram, Krishna, Kalki.

Matsya Purana too mentions ten incarnations namely Yajna, Narasimha, Vaman Dattatreya, Mandhata, Jamadagna, Ram, Vedavyasa, Buddha, Kalki.

Number of incarnations given in Agni Purana is ten such as Matsya, Kurma, Varaha, Narasimha, Vamana, Parashuram, Ram, (Bala) Ram, Buddha, Kalki.

Vaupurana gives out names of ten incarnations including Yajna, Narasimha, Vamana (Upendra), Datta, Mandhata, Jamadagna, Ram, Vedavyasa, Krishna and Kalki.

Brahmapurana says that Vishnu's incarnation were eight in number. They were Varaha, Nrisimha, Vamana, Datta, Jamadagna, Ram, Krishna and Kalki. In the fifth canto of Padmapurana, there is elaborate description of ten incarnations of Vishnu such as Matsya, Varaha, Vamana, Ram, Kalki, Kurma, Narasimha, Parashurama, Krishna, Buddha.

In the Skanda Purana's Vaishnava Khanda we find the number of incarnation as fourteen. They are Varaha, Matsya, Kurma, Narasimha, Vamana, Kapil, Datta, Rishabha, Parashuram, Dasharathi Ram, Krishna, Vyas, Buddha, Kalki.

Vishnu Purana says that there were seven incarnations of Vishnu including Yajna, Ajit, Satya, Hari, Manas,

Vaikuntha and Vamana. Vishnudharmottara gives out fourteen names. They are Narasimha, Varaha, Kapil, Vishvarupa, Hayagriva, Padmanabha, Vamana, Kurma, Hamsa, Matsya, Dattatreya, Mohini, Pruthu, Bhargava Ram, Dasharathi Ram, Valmiki.

Shrimadbhagavata at three places gives three different lists on names numbering twenty two, twentythree and fifteen. However the list of ten incarnations given in the Jayadeva's 12th century work Gita Govinda is generally accepted. This list mentions the names of Meena, Kacchapa, Shukara, Narahari (Narasimha), Vamana, Bhrugupati (Parashuram), Ram (Dasharathi), Haladhara (Balarma), Buddha, Kalki. In this list the name of Krishna does not occur because according to one tradition it was Krishna who took all these incarnations. Hence Jayadeva says Dashakritikrute Krishnaya tubhyam namah!

It was generally accepted that Vishnu's incarnations were ten. In his treatise on theatrical arts, Dasharupaka, written around last quarter of tenth century Acharya Dhanajaya says that:

दझारूपानुकारेण यस्य माद्यन्ति भावकाः।
नमः सर्वविदे तस्मै विष्णवे भरताय च॥

The number of forms of drama, according to Bharata, the author of Natyashastra, ascribed to the period between B.C. 200 to A.D. 200, was ten. So are the incarnations of Vishnu. Hence in this verse Dhananjaya bringing out this similarity pays obeisance to Bharata and Vishnu the creator of ten forms. However Acharya Dhananjaya did not mention the exact names of ten incarnations he had in his mind. Probably Jayadeva highlighted these ten names of Vishnu's incarnations as per earlier dramatic tradition.

Around 12th century Acharya Nandikeshvara wrote his treatise on dramatic acting named Abhinayadarpana. In his treatise the Acharya enlists Hasta-mudras, hand gestures, to indicate ten incarnations on the stage while dancing. He states :

DASHAVATAR

दशावतारहस्ताः

मत्स्यावतार	मत्स्यहस्तं दर्शयित्वा ततः स्कन्धसमौ करौ । धृतौ मत्स्यावतारस्य हस्त इत्यभिघीयते ।।
कूर्मावतार	कूर्महस्तं दर्शयित्वा ततः स्कन्धसमौ करौ । धृतौ कूर्मावतारस्य हस्त इत्याभिघीयते ।।
वराहावतार	दर्शयित्वा वराहं तु कटिपार्श्वसमौ करौ । धृतौ वराहावतारस्य देवस्य कर इष्यते ।।
नृसिंहावतार	वामे सिंहमुखं धृत्वा दक्षिणे त्रिपताकिकाम् । नरसिंहावतारस्य हस्त इत्युच्यते बुधैः ।।
वामनावतार	ऊर्ध्वाधो धृतमुष्टिभ्यां सव्यान्याभ्यां यदि स्थितः । स वामनावतारस्य हस्त इत्यभिधीयते ।।
परशुरामावतार	वामं कटितटे न्यस्य दक्षिणेऽर्धपताकिका । धृतौ परशुरामस्य हस्त इत्यभिघीयते ।।
रामचन्द्रवतार	कपित्थो दक्षिणे हस्ते वामे तु शिखरः करः । उर्ध्व धृतो रामचन्द्रहस्त इत्युच्यते बुधैः ।।
बलरामावतार	पताको दक्षिणे हस्ते मुष्टिर्वामकरे तथा । बलरामावतारस्य हस्त इत्युच्यते बुधैः ।।
कृष्णावतार	मृगशीर्षे तु हस्ताभ्यामन्योन्याभिमुखे कृते । आस्योपकण्ठे कृष्णस्य हस्त इत्युच्यते बुधैः ।।
कल्कि अवतार	पताको दक्षिणे वामे त्रिपताकः करो धृतः । कल्क्याख्यस्यावतारस्य हस्त इान्यभिधीयते ।।

Verses 216 to 225

HASTA MUDRAS

Matsya Hasta Mudra : One palm on another, both pointing downwards, both the thumbs and little fingers spread out, hands at shoulder height. (216, 196).

Kurma : All fingers extended straight and joined together is *Patak Hasta Mudra.* When the thumb of *Patak Hasta* is separated and extended out it is *Ardhachandra Hasta.* Both palms in *Ardhachandra* joined together freeing little finger and thumb is *Kurma Hasta* (93, 197, 217) Hands at shoulder height.

Varaha : The middle of the *Pataka* hand is hollowed, thumb and little finger extended is *Mrigashirsha,* both the palms in *Mrigashirsha,* little finger of one *MS* touching thumb of another *MS.* (139, 198, 218).

Nrusimha : The tips of the middle and the third fingers are applied to the thumbs and the rest extended is *Simha Mukha* (142). Right hand in *SM Mudra* and left in *Tripatak Mudra.* When third finger of *Patak* is bent it is *Tripatak.* (142, 100, 219).

Vamana : The four fingers are bent into the palm and the thumb is set on them is *Mushti* (fist), when one fist is held above another it is *Vamana* (16, 220).

Prashuram : Left hand on hips,and right in *Ardha Patak.* A little finger of *Tripatak* is also bent is *Ardhapatak* (103, 221).

Rama : Left hand is *Kapittha Mudra* and right in *Shikhar Mudra.* If the thumb of *Mushti* is raised it, is *Shikhara.* The forefinger of the *Shikhara* hand is bent over the top of the thumb is *Kapittha*—elephant apple. (118, 121, 222).

Balaram	:	Right hand in *Patak* and left in *Mushti Hasta Mudra* (223).
Krishna	:	Both the hands in *Mrigashirsha* facing each other; held in front of the mouth (224).

The Sarasvati Mahal library of Tanjore which was established by Maratha king Maharaja Sarfoji published a book Sri Nrityalalshanasahitam Gitagovinda Mahakavyam under the title Gita Govinda with Abhinaya. The work translated each and every word of the poem into dramatic action. It is believed that this work belongs to Bharatnatyam tradition and was probably written by the direct disciple of Jayadeva himself or those just after him.

The symbolic gestures of showing ten incarnations of Krishna are thus mentioned :

Krishna	:	Vaishnavasthanakena Vamshad-haranamudraya
Meena	:	Makarahastakena
Kacchapa	:	Shukatundena
Sukara	:	Tamrachudabhyam or Mukhalagnakanishtikashikharena
Narahari	:	Skandhamuladarshitalapallavena Swastikikritapulas talornanabhabhyam
Bhrugupati	:	Not given
Vamana	:	Talantari todharvadhas talarghachandrabhyam
Rama	:	Avadhutena shirasa lalatasthaanjalina
Haladhara	:	Skandhasthitaralena
Buddha	:	Stabdhasirasa
Kalki	:	Manibandhagatakartarimukhena turangamacharya.

Depiction of Vishnu's Dashavataras or ten incarnation is a favourite item in the repertory of major classical dance forms of India. The Mukti Mangal Bhatima or opening prayer song of one of the plays of Mahapurusha Shankardeva in Ankia Nat style written in 16th century has a theme of Dashavatara. Dashavatari folk plays are enacted in the temples of Goa and Konkan area of Maharashtra. The Yakshagana plays of Karnataka too are alternatively known as Dhshavatar Ata. Traditional theatrical forms that evolved in different parts of the country stage plays based on all or any one Incarnations of Vishnu.

Jagar is oldest extant dramatic form of Gomantaka. Basically it presents the story of Vishnu killing the demons Madhu and Kaitabha. According to Natyashastra of Bharata the Lord killed the demons with 'varid pure expressive and graceful angaharas.' The vrittis emerged out of this combat (NS 22. 1-16). Angahara means body movements pertaining to dance. Angahara is a bigger dance posture made up of smaller units known as Karanas.

Vishnu, members of his immediatel family circle, his manifestations and incarnations were known to common folk around the beginning of Christian era. King Hal Satavahana of Pratishthan collected some seven hundred Maharashtri Prakrit verses, Gathas, in the first or second century A.D. and the collection became famous as Gatha Saptashati. Number of Shaiva and Vaishnava deities are mentioned in this unique collection of verses reflecting romance of folk life.

Interestingly the name Vishnu does not occur even for once in this collection. Instead he is referred to as Hari, his yet another name. One verse without directly mentioning Hari or Vishnu is dedicated to him. It says : I bow before Him who is wearing dazzling Kaustubha jem in a pendant falling on his chest. In it is reflected the face of beautiful Lakshmi as if the spotless moon get reflected in a disk of Sun.

It is believed that here is a suggestion of Viparita rati, woman on the top of man, as poet suggests that the reflection of Lakshmi's face who is making love to Vishnu in inverted position naturally gets reflected in a jem on the chest of her lord.

Another verse says : 'While making love to Hari in inverted posture, Viparita rati, Lakshmi suddenly noticed the presence of Brahma sitting in a lotus sprouted from the navel of her lord. The bashful lady closed the right eye of her lover.

The verse is based on the belief that when Hari closed his right eye night falls. At the fall of the night the petals of lotus flower closes engulfing Brahma in them, oblitering his presence.

The Vaman incarnation of Hari is mentioned in a few verses, some of them with erotic hidden meaning.

A verse says : 'Madhumathana assuming the form of Vamala grew in size and overcome Bali. Likewise her small breasts grew is size (with age) and overcome the trivali.

Trivali or three delicate folds on the stomach of a beautiful girl are considered as signs of beauty. Her boosoms grew to such proportion that they obliterated the trivali as Vamana did to Bali. Here is an interesting interplay on the words Bali and tri-vali.

A verse says : 'The earth could not contain the third feet of Hari (in his two strides he covered earth and Patala) hence it went to sky. There it was adorned by the luminious stars as if those were flowers. I bow before the Hari whose feet was adorned with flowers of star.

This verse do not mention the word Vamana, instead he is called as Hari. Later Bhasyakaras connected this rather innocuous verse to an erotic posture used while making love, known as Trivikrambandha. In this bandha girl lifts her one leg up taking the support of arm of her lover while standing and makes love to him. In this posture two legs of standing man and one of his female partner (one being lifted up) root firmly on the earth or ground. They look like 'tripadatvan Harih Vishnuh Vamanarupah' or Vamana with his three strides or having three legs.

In the Panchasayaka this bandha is called Tripadbandha, bandha based on three legs. In the Nagarasarvasva written by Buddhistmonk Padmashri this posture is called Harivikrama Asana. The uplifted leg of the girl looks as if Vamana has lifted his one leg to occupy Swarga, Mrityu and Patala – threefold division of earth. Vatsyayana calls the act of love making, both partners standing, as Sthitarata. Vatsyayana's Kamasutra belongs to third century A.D. while other two works, Panchasayaka and Nagarsarvasva, were written around 10th century A.D.

There is a passing reference to Rama and his brother Lakshmana in a verse in this collection. But it seems that Krishna story was more popular. In Baudhayana Dharma Sutra, ascribed to fourth century B.C., one of the names of Vishnu is given as Damodara. Damodara means one who has a cord around his belly. It was a practice among cowherd men to tie such cord around the stomach. In one of the Gathas Krishna is referred to as Damodara. The verse says : 'When mother Yashoda pleaded with young cowherd girls (who have come to her to complain about Krishna's flirtious ways and naughty acts) that boy Damodara is a mere child as yet, the young gopis threw a glance/at Krishna and laughed among themselves.'

Scriptures, Puranas, epics, literary works contributed to the evolution of Avatara theme by creating new myths, stories, episodes in abundance. Gatha Saptashati too is not exception to this. It is for the first time name of cowherd beloved of Krishna, Radha, appears in one of the Gathas included in the book. It says: 'It was evening time. Cows were returning home. Dust was raised by their movements. Dust particles affected the beautiful eyes of Radha.Chivalrous Krishna came forward to remove the cow-dust from her eyes by the puff of his mouth (and probaly kissed her on that pretext ?). Thus Krishna hurt the ego of young jealous cowherd girls standing around them.'

Later poets picked up the Radha myth from the Gatha and enlarged it, Gita Govinda of Jayadeva being the best example of this.

Gatha Saptashati betrays the knowledge of the Mahabharata war also. In this context one verse addresses Krishna-Vishnu as Madhava.

2

MATSYA

Matsya, Fish, is the very first incarnation of Vishnu. Jayadeva in his Dashavatara Ashtapadi in the Gita Govinda says :

When during great deluge

Vedas went down in troubled waters

You took the form of Fish to rescue them

O Keshava, victory to you Jagadisha Hare

Acharya Nandikeshvara in his work Abhinaya Darpana while explaining hand gesture to indicate Matsya Avatara says :

One palm on another, both pointing downward, both the thumbs and little fingers spread out, hands at shoulder hight.

Padma Purana says : Brahma created nine Prajapatis. One among them Marici gave birth to Kashyapa. Kashyapa had four wives. Aditi gave birth to gods and Diti cruel Asuras.

Diti's son Makara was very powerful. He went to Brahmaloka and took away all the four Vedas from him. He then entered the vast waters of ocean.

In the absence of Vedas the Dharma disappeared from the earth. Frightened by this development all the gods led by Brahma went to Vishnu at his abode in Milky Ocean, Kshirasagara.

Listening to their woes Vishnu took the form of a fish and entered the ocean. He then killed the terrible demon Makara and brought back the Vedas.

Another version of this incarnation is for the first time found in the Shatapatha Brahmana followed by Mahabharata, Ramayana, Matsya Purana, Agni Purana, Kurma Purana, Vishnu Purana and Bhagavata Purana. Let us follow the Matsya story in the Mahabharata.

Vivasvan (Sun) had a handsome son who was great Maharshi and in brightness equal to Prajapatis. He performed severe penance at Badarikashrama standing on one leg and lifting one hand above his head for ten thousand years. He became famous as Vaivasvata Manu.

One day he was doing penance on the bank of river Chirini a small fish came to him and requested him to save from bigger ones who eat them.

Showing mercy on him Manu took him home and kept in earthern pot. He started growing at fast pace. One day the fish told him that he has outgrown the earthern pot, so Manu put him in a big well. The fish continued to grow, Manu transferred him to river Ganga and from there to ocean. Meanwhile he became really big.

One day he told Manu that soon great deluge is going to come which will drawn all the world, hence built a sturdy boat and sit in it along with Saptarshis and the seeds of all creatures. At appropriate time he would come to him. He would recognise him by the horn on his head.

And indeed great deluge came. Manu started floating on the sea on his boat. He remembered the great fish and he did arrive. Meanwhile he had grown to the size of big mountain and had a horn on his head.

Manu tied the boat with rope to the horn of the great fish and they remain floating for several years. When the flood started receeding the great fish asked Manu to fasten the boat to the one of the peaks of Himalays.

Manu did what the great fish asked him to do. Gradually dry land appeared. The great fish asked him to start the work of creating the world anew. The great fish told him that he was none but Prajapati Brahma himself.

Though Mahabharata identified the great fish as Prajapati Brahma, other Puranas, including Bhagavata Purana, declared him to be the incarnation of Lord Vishnu.

To this Bhagavata Purana adds that a demon named Hayagriva stole the Vedas from Brahma. Lord Vishnu took Matsya incarnation and after killing the demon returned the Vedas to Brahma.

Folk dramatic performances in Gomantaka and Konkan area of Maharashtra known as Dashavatari Natak most prominently enacts the Matsyavatar episode. Here the name of demon who stole the Vedas is given out as Shankhasur who acts as a villain and jester rolled into one. In the end Vishnu kills him and rescue the Vedas.

N.P. Joshi in his Bharatiya Murtishastra writes that we do not find independant images or temples of Matsya, Kurma and Kalki incarnations of Vishnu till Gupta period. In medieval period we find a few images of Matsya incarnation. In one style a fish having two human hands is sculpted as Matsyavatar and in another Vishnu having four arms is shown emerging out of fish with Lakshmi and Saraswati by his side.

3

KURMA

Samudra Manthan or the legend of churning of ocean by gods and demons to obtain Amrita, elixir of life, is one of the major myth that occurs in the epics and Puranas. In it is weaved an interesting tale of fourth tortoise (Kurma).

Seeds of the myths regarding two incarnations of Vishnu are found in the Brahmanas. It is said in the Shatapatha Brahmana that 'Prajapati about to create off-spring becomes a tortoise moving in the premeval waters.' In some Puranas this tortoise is an incarnation of Vishnu in the Samudra Manthan legend.

Shatapatha Brahmana says : 'The Lord of Progeny, having assumed the form of tortoise, created off spring. He made the whole creation, hence the name Deed (Kurma) given to tortoise.

Jayadeva in his Dashavatar Astapadi or poem describing ten incarnations of Krishna writing about Kacchapa,that is tortoise incarnation, says :

You carried the vast earth on your back

That left deep marks there

O Keshava in tortoise form

Victory to you Jagadisha Hare

About showing Kurma Hasta Mudra indicating tortoise incarnation on stage while enacting ten incarnations of Vishnu, Acharya Nandikeshvara in his Abhinayadarpana says :

> All fingers extended straight and joined together is Patak Hasta Mudra. When the thumb of Patak Hasta is seperated and extended out it is Ardhachandra Hasta. Both palms in Ardhachandra joined together freeing little finger and thumb is Kurma Hasta to be held forward at shoulder High.

It is in the Mahabharata the Samudra Manthan story appeared for the first time. It said:

Once upon a time all deities assembled on the peak of Meru mountain to deliberate upon as to how Amrita should be obtained. Bhagavan Narayana told Brahma and other deities that they along with Asuras, or demons churn the great ocean for obtaining the elixir of life. They should continue chursing the ocean till they get what they desired, he advised.

They decided to make Mandarachal mountain churning rod. Bhagavan Vishnu asked the great serpent Ananta (on whose coils he sleeps) to uproot the great mountain and bring it on the shore of ocean.

The gods and demons requested Kurmaraj, great tortoise lying at the bottom of the ocean, to support the churning rod, Mandarachala, from below and save it from drawning.

Then gods and demons started churning the ocean. Things like Moon, Lakshmi, Suradevi, white horses, jem Kaustubha (Parijata wish fulfilling tree and Surabhi cow) appear from the ocean. Kaustubha adorned the chest of Bhagavan Narayana and all other things went to heaven where gods lived.

In the end Dhanvantari appeared holding the white pot full of Amrita. He was followed by great elephant Airavata and deadly poison Kalakata. On the request of Brahma to save the world from getting destroyed Lord Shiva drank it and held it in his throat which became blue due to its effect.

Demons started clamouring for Lakshmi and Amrita and for these two things became enemy of gods.

By using his Maya, power of illusion, Narayana took the form of most beautiful woman, Mohini and went to demons. Coming under her influence gods and demons handed over the Amrita to her. She served it to gods ignoring demons.

When gods were drinking Amrita, a demon named Rahu entered their rank in the guise of a deity. Bhagavan cut his head with the help of Sudarshana Chakra. As the Amrita had reached his throat he became immortal. As Moon and Sun exposed him he became their sworn enemy.

There ensured great fight among gods and demons. Two forms of Vishnu, Nara and Narayana, appeared in the battlefield. Nara with his bow and arrows and Narayana with his Chakra started killing demons. As they could not endure the onslought of gods led by Nara and Narayana entered the earth and the salty water of the ocean.

Though in this account in the Mahabharata Mohini is described as an manifestation of Narayana, the great tortoise, Kurmaraj, is not linked to him. However it was in the epic Ramayana it is said that when mountain Mandara which became churing rod, started sinking in the ocean the gods requested Bhagavan Madhusudana to save the situation took the form of tortoise and gave it support from below.Vishvatma Purushottam Bagavan Keshava firmly held the upper portion of the mountain with his hand and made the mountain stable.

Number of interesting versions of the story are found mentioned in different Puranas. Most of the Puranas, including Padma and Bhagavata, tell us that Vishnu took the Kurma incarnation to support the Mandarachal from below during the churning of the sea.

However the Linga Purana states that when the earth started sinking Vishnu manifested as Kurma and held her firmly on his back. In the Dashavatara Ashtapadi Jayadeva refers to this episode.

N.P. Joshi in his Bharatiya Murtishastra has referred to some Kurma images. He says there are three types of Kurma images. In the first a simple tortoise is shown. In the second the episode of churning of the ocean is depicted. In this scene we see Kurma bearing on his back the Mandara mountain encircled by Vasuki. In the third type instead of Mandara we see Shiva linga.

Samudra manthan myth is intended to establish greatness of Vishnu.

4

VARAHA

Varaha, boar, incarnation of Vishnu charged with immense vigour and strength became a sort of cult figure which was translated into colossal and awe inspiring sculptures found at many places in the country.

Jayadeva in his Dashavatara Ashtapadi says :

> The earth you lifted up placing it on your teeth
>
> Looks like dark spot on the moon
>
> O Keshava in boar form
>
> Victory to you Jagadisha Hare!

About showing Varaha Hasta Mudra on the stage by the dancer Acharya Nandikeshvara in his Abhinaya Darpana says :

> The middle of the pataka hand is hollowed, thumb and little finger extended is Mrigashirsha, both the palms in Mrigashirsha, little finger of one Mrigashirsha touching finger of another Mrigashirsha.

Varaha finds mention in the Rig Veda and allied literature in different contexts. Macdonell in his Vedic Mythology states :

> 'Another myth of the Brahmanas (about boar) has its origin in two passages of the Rig Veda. Their purport is that Vishnu having drunk Soma and being urged by Indra, carried off hundred buffaloes and brew of milk belonging to the boar (= Vritra) while Indra shooting across the (cloud) mountain slew the fierce (emusara) boar. The myth in the Taittiriya Samhita developed as follows. A boar, the plunderer of wealth,

> kept the goods of Asuras on the other side of seven hills. Indra plucking up a bunch of kusa grass and piercing through these hills slew the boar. Vishnu, the sacrifice, carried the boar off as a sacrifice for the gods. So the gods obtained the goods of the Asuras. In the corresponding passage of the Kathaka the boar is called Emusa. The same story with slight variations is told in the Charaka Brahmana (quoted by Syana). This boar appears in the cosmogonic character in the Shatapatha Brahmana, where under the name of Emusa he is stated to have raised up the earth from waters. In the Taittiriya Samhita this cosmogonic boar, which raised the earth from the priemeval waters, is described as a form of Prajapati. This modification of the myth is further expanded in the Taittiriya Brahmana. In the post Vedic mythology of the Ramayana and the Puranas, the boar which raises the earth, has become one of the Avataras of Vishnu, (p. 41).

It is said in the Taittiriya Samhita that before the emergence of earth Prajapati was moving in the Antariksha in the form of Vayu, wind. One of his wanderings he saw the earth submerged in the waters of ocean. Prajapati, assuming the form of a boar entered the ocean and lifted the earth out of it.

Taittiriya Brahmana saya, 'the lord of creation practiced austerities, (wondering : 'How should this (universe) be? He saw a lotus leaf standing and thought : 'This lotus must rest on something.' Assuming the shape of a boar, he dived beneath and found the earth. Breaking off a fragment, he rose to the surface and spread it on lotus leaf. As he spread it, it became something that is spread. Hence is the earth called' that-which-became (Bhumi).

Versions of Varaha myth are found in different Puranas. The Bhagavata Purana says :

Brahma asked Swayambhuva Manu and his wife Shatarupa to produce children took up the administration of mother earth, Prithvi, and rule it according to tenets of Dharma and worship Srihari through Yajna.

Manu replied that he would certainly obey him but where was the place for my progeny to live ? Due to great deluge the Prithvi had submerged in water.

As Brahma was thinking about the ways of taking Prithvi out of waters from his nostril emerged a Varaha-shishu of the size of a thumb. He grew fast and assumed the size of an elephant. Brahma and Rishis thought that he must have been none else but Bhagavan Yajnapurusha himself. Meanwhile the Varaha grew to the size of a mountain and started roaring. Moving like huge elephant he entered the waters of ocean. His body was very hard which was covered with stiff rock-like hair and had white jaw and firm horn.

When he entered the ocean the water parted by his action and sound of terrible thunder filled the sky. After locating the Prithvi he lifted her on his white teeth and started emerging out of water.

To obstruct his ascent the great demon Hiranyaksha attacked him in the water with his mace. This made the Varaha very angry and killed the demon as lion kills elephant.

When Varaha Bhagavan, having complexion as blue as Tamala tree, emerged from the waters balancing earth on his white teeth Brahma and other Munigana had no doubt about he being Bhagavan himself and they started offering him prayers.

Prajapati Bhagavan Srihari placed the earth on the surface of the waters of ocean and disappeared.

About Hiranyaksha the Bhagavata Purana says : Diti, daughter of Daksha Prajapati, with the desire to be get a son requested her husband Kashyapa, son of Marichi to make love to her though it was eveing time, forbidden by Shastras for such act.

Marichi could not resist his wife and fell prey to her entreaty. However he warned her that as a result of her act she would give birth to two extremely cruel sons who would inflict untold misery on people. Ultimately Bhagavan Vishveshvara would take incarnation and kill them.

Vishnu's two attendants, Jaya and Vijaya, cursed by the sages for refusing them entry in inner chamber of the deity, took birth on the earth as demon sons of Diti named Hiranyaksha and Hiranyakashipu.

Varahabhagavan killed Hiranyaksha and for eliminating Hiranyakashipu he took Narasimha, half-man half-man incarnation.

Brahma Purana narrates different legend about Varaha incarnation of Lord Vishnu. It says : Once upon a time a demon named Sindhusena defeated the gods and ran away with Yajna. with it he entered into Rasatala, region below the earth. Indra and other gods followed him but could not get the Yajna back. Hence they all went to Puranapurusha Bhagavan Vishnu. He assuming the form of Varaha went after the demon. After killing him he rescued the Yajna. He then leaving the netherworld emerged from the Ganga river. The spot from where he came up in the river became famous as Varaha tirtha. One who takes bath in river Ganga at Varaha tirtha gets the merit, punya, of performing all the Yajnas or Vedic fire sacrifices.

In addition to Taittiriya Aranyaka and Taittiriya Samhita,the Taittiriya Brahmana and the Shatapatha Brahmana mentions Varaha myth. It is also found in the Mahabharata, the Vishnu Dharmottara Purana, the Padma Purana, the Vayu Purana, the Agni Purana, the Brahma Purana, the Linga Purana, the Kurma Purana as well as in the Vishnu Purana (Danielou).

In the Western group of Khajuraho temples there is a shrine dedicated to Varaha incarnation of Vishnu. 'It contains profusely carved standing image of gigantic Varaha, highly polished. Ascribed to A.T. 950-1002 it is a marvellous animal sculpture.' In the Varadarajswami Vishnu temple complex at Kanchi there is a dialapidated shrine dedicated to Varaha. It is empty as the Varaha image is removed to the interior of the temple.

G.N. Mohapatra in his Jagannatha in History and Religious Traditions of Orissa writes : 'It is known from Rajim Mahatmya that there were Shaiva and Vaishnava shrines at Rajim. The presiding deity Rajibalocana is surrounded by the group of temples dedicated to Varaha, Narasimha, Badrinatha, Vamana and Jagannatha. Cunnigham assigns these temples to about fifth century A.D.' (p. 33).

Mohapatra further informs that in the 16th century A.D. great Orissan king Prataparudradeva, builder of audience hall of Jagannatha temple at Puri, built a Varaha (Vishnu) temple at Yajpur (p. 74).

N.P. Joshi in his Bharatiya Murtishastra tells us that we start getting the images of Varaha from Kushana period. One such image is housed in Mathura Museum having human body and head of Varaha (now broken). It has at its feet an broken inscription in Brahmi.

We start getting Varaha images in large number since Gupta period. Some of them are having the head of Varaha and human body. Such images are called Nruvaraha. Varaha images in fully animal form are known as Yajna Varaha. In some Varaha images Lakshmi is seen sitting on his lap.

Nruvaraha images are known as Mahavaraha and Bhuvaraha also. It is said that one who worships Varaha gets kingdom of the earth.Varaha was insignia of Royal Rashtrakuta dynasty.

In central India number of Varaha images were found. A colossal image of Varaha having human body and the head of boar, ascribed to Gupta period, can be seen at Udayagiri, Bhopal. He is carrying Privthvi in a female form on his teeth. During the reign of Kalachuri dynasty huge Varaha images were established at many places including Karitlai, Mazoli, Rithi, Bilhari, Panagar, Nohata, Madanpur, Harada.

In the lucknow Museum there is a Varaha image in fully animal form standing on four legs.

There is a Varaha Upanishada attached to Krishna Yajurveda. It contains the discourse of Brahmavidya narrated by Varaha Vishnu to Ribhu Rishi. We also find Varaha Purana which is considered as Mahapurana. This Purana was narrated by Varaha Vishnu to Prithvi. In the opening verse prayer is offered to Varaha who had lifted earth out of water – Namastasmai Varahaya lilayoddha rate mahim.

There is a place called Varaha tirtha near Nathapur in Bengal. It is said that it was at this place Varaha lifted earth out of water. Devotees observe Varaha-dwadashi on Magha Shuddha Dwadashi when golden image of Varaha is given to Brahmana. Observance of this Vrata makes a person lucky, wealthy, beautiful and is blessed with son.

In Puranic mythology Prithvi, the mother goddess earth, is described as consort of Vishnu, particularly in his Varaha, boar, incarnation. May be because the great boar lifted her out of deep waters in which she was submerged.

Prithvi is dified in the Vedas. Hymns dedicated to her are found in the Rig Veda and Atharva Veda. Macdonell in his Vedic Mythology says : 'The personification is but slight, the attributes of the goddess being chiefly those of physical earth. According to the Rig Veda she abounds in hights, bears the burden of mountains, and supports the trees of the forests in ground. She is great, firm and shining. Prithvi is spoken of as 'Kindly Mother Earth', to whom the dead man in the funeral hymn is exorted to go.'

In the Vedas She makes couple with Dyaus, the sky. But in later Puranic literature she, the Bhu Devi, is consort of Vishnu along with Sri Devi, Lakshmi.

It is stated in the Vishnu Purana (V. 29, 23) that Prithvi had a son named Narakasura, from Vishnu in his boar incarnation. Kalika Purana has elaborated upon this myth. Narakasura had his capital, Pragjyotishpur, situated on the Varaha mountain.

5

NARASIMHA

Narasimha or Man-Lion-Incarnation of Vishnu is one of the major manifestations of Supreme Lord. Among all creatures man is the most powerful and excellent and among beasts the lion. The combination of the two in one body represent fierce strength, courage and intellect, which was required to vanquish evil forces plaguing the earth.

Describing this terrible incarnation poet Jayadeva in his famous Dashavatara Ashtapadi says :

> The fingers of your lotus hands have wonderfully sharp nails
>
> By which you tore the body of Hiranyakashipu
>
> O Keshava in Man-lion form
>
> Victory to you Jagadisha Hare

Acharya Nandikeshvara in his Abhinayadarpana instructing the dancers about how to show Narasimha by hand gesture states :

> The tips of the middle and third fingers are applied to the thumbs and rest extended is Simha Mukha. When the third finger in Patak is bent it is Tripatak. Right hand in Simha Mukha Mudra and left should be in Tripatak mudra.

According to Bharatiya Prachin Charitra Kosha it seems that the concept of Narasimha emerged from Indra-Namuchi fight recorded in some hymns of the Rig Veda and from there it spread to Brahmana works. In the Taittiriya Aranyaka (10.1.7, 16) there is a mention of Narasimha incarnation. There is one Upanishada by name Nrisimhatapini.

Shiva is known as Pashupati, Lord of the beasts. In the Anushashana Parva of the Mahabharata it is said that Shiva moves around assuming the forms of different animals, one among them being a lion.

Bhagavata Purana says that demon Hiranyakashipu was brother of demon Hiranyakshya who was slain by Vishnu in his Varaha incarnation. Hiranyakashipu with the intention of becoming master of the world and attain immortality started performing severe penance in one of the caves of mountain Mandarachala.

Brahma, pleased, by his penance appeared before him and asked him to ask for any boon he desires.

As a boon Hiranyakashipu demanded that he should not be killed by anybody of his creation — may he be a human, animal, demon or divinity, by day or by night, inside or outside of his residence, by weapons or missiles, in the sky or on the earth. The demon asked him to grant him the kingdom of the earth.

By dint of the boons granted by Brahma the demon became so powerful that he conquered entire universe and started living in the palace of Indra, king of gods, enjoying the dances of heavenly damsels, Apsaras. Drinking wine with strong fragrances he indulged in all kinds of pleasures of senses.

Depressed gods started offering prayers to Bhagavan Srihari requesting him to redeem them from the tyranny of the cruel demon. One day they heard the divine voice coming from the sky which said that whosoever starts troubling and hating gods, Vedas, Brahmins, Saints, Dharma and himself soon meets his end. They need not worry. He would himself vanquish the demon.

Pleased to hear this divine announcement, Akashavani, the gods went home.

Hiranyakashipu had four sons, Prahlad being the youngest. He was a gentle soul and repository of good qualities. He was great devotee of Srikrishna. One day father asked the son about how his education was proceeding? Prahlada sang the praise of Vishnu, the sworn enemy of the family, and defined the path of Bhakti. He said :

Sravanam kirtanam Vishnowh

Smaranam padasevanam

Archanam vandanam dasyam

Sakhyamatmanivedanam.

The nine ingredients of Bhakti according to Prahlada were :

Shravana	:	Listening to the names and acts (Lila) of Vishnu
Kirtana	:	Reciting, singing, mentioning, repeating the names and deeds of Vishnu.
Smarana	:	Constantly remembering Vishnu
Padasevanam	:	Serving his divine feet
Archana	:	Honouring, praising, paying homage to Vishnu
Vandana	:	Praise, worship, adoration
Dasya	:	To become his servent, slave
Sakhya	:	Close affinity
Atmanivedana	:	Expressing one's innermost thoughts feelings, desires. Confession.

All his adoration of Vishnu infuriated the demon. He ordered his followers to kill Prahlada immediately.

They attacked him with spears, tried to crush him under the feet of elephant, bitten by poisonous serpents, let loose on him demonic spirits (kritya), threw him down from the mountains, Sambarasura tried every trick in his book, impersoned him in dark prison chamber, made him drink poison, stopped giving him food, placed him in ice cold chamber, put him on fire, dropped him in ocean, tried to crush him under the hills and mountains but nothing worked as he was protected by Vishnu.

Desperate Hiranyakashipu, the all powerful demon, called his son in his presence. After rebuking him severely he asked him where his Jagadishvar was? If he was everywhere as he said he must be in this pillar of the palace also, he said sarcastically.

Blinded by rage Hiranyakashipu jumped down his throne and gave a severe blow by his hand to the pillar.

Then everybody present there heard a terrible sound. From the pillar emerged a terrible creature who was neither a man nor the beast. Taking the frightening form of Narasimha, divinity with human body and the head of a lion, he stood before the demon.

Angry demon attacked him with all ferocity. After playing with him for a while he caught the demon as cobra catches the mouse. He sat on the threshold of his court and with his sharp nails tore his stomach by placing him on his lap.

But according to Brahma Purana Narasimha story does not end here. It says in his furious frenzy Narasimha moved all over the world killing demons, Daityas and Asuras. At the end he arrived at the bank of river Gautami (Godavari), the giver of joy to mind and eyes, and one who had its origin from the feet of the Lord himself. There lived a demon named Ambarya who was the ruler of Dandakaranya. Even gods could not contain him. He had a large army. Srihari in his Narasimha incarnation in a terrible fight vanquished the demon and his invincible army.

He did this on the north shore of the river. The place where he did this became famous as Narasimha Tirtha. The Purana says as Vishnu is supreme among gods so is Narasimha Tirtha among sacred places of pilgrimage. One who takes bath in this Tirtha gets rid of his sins, is protected from old age and death and all other troubles. The man who takes bath here and worships Narasimha is sure to enjoy all the pleasures of Swarga, Martyalok and Patala.

This Purana states that Narasimha lives in Purushottama Kshetra that is Puri on seashore. It then very elaborately speaks about Narasimha Mahatmya.

According to a folk legend Hiranyakashipu had a sister named Holika. She was very cruel and could endure fire. She volunteered to kill Prahlada. Taking advantage of her being kind of fire-proof she decided to sit on a pile of fire-wood along with Prahlada and ignate it. When she sat in the fire holding Prahlada by grace of Vishnu he came out unscathed but the demoness was consumed by fire.

This legend got associated with the festival of bonfire, Holi, which is celebrated on Phalguna Purnima in North India.

In the Braj region of Uttar Pradesh there is a tiny village named Phalen, corrupt form of Prahlad. Here on the bank of a tank, known as Prahlad Kunda, there is a small temple of Prahlada. Here the enactment Prahlada-Holika story takes place around Holi.

A huge pile of fire-wood is made in between Prahlada Kunda and the temple of Prahlada. It is torched in the night and it bursts forth with tremendous blaze, fire leaping to the sky. Jumping, dancing and brandishing canes the youth of the village move around the fire. Then the priest of the temple takes holy bath in the tank and rush through the great orb of fire, unharmed. He represents Prahlada himself in the fire-ordeal of Phalen.

In Orissa there is a form of folk drama named Prahlada Nataka is enacted depicting Narasimha legend. At Melattur in the Tamilnadu on the occasion of Narasimha Jayanti a play named Prahlada, Natakam is enacted as a part of the festival of Varadaraja.

The myth is indeed very dramatic and eminently suitable as a theme for a performance. There are as many Narasimha sculptures all over India as there are dramatic forms which have adopted this theme for theatrical performance.

A Telugu Brahmin named Narayana Tirtha Yati who had settled in a village in Tanjore district of Tamil Nadu started a dramatic tradition in the later half of 16th century which came to be known as Bhagavata Mela. His famous composition is 'Krishna Leela Tarangini' which he wrote in Sanskrit. He also wrote a number of dance-dramas in Telugu, the most famous among them is 'Parijatapaharanam' or the story of the conquest of Parijata Tree. The tradition continued to flourish under the Nayak and Maratha royal patronage. However, it was Gopala Krishna Shastri and his illustrious son Venkatarama Shastriar who gave real boost to this art by composing numerous dance-dramas while living at Melatpur near Tanjavur around one hundred and fifty years ago. One of the most famous of these dance-dramas is 'Prahlad Natakam' which is based on the Narasimha myth. Written by Venkatarama Shastriar this drama is still enacted on the occasion of Narasimha-jayanti festival of Varadraja temple at Melatur. In the temple there is an idol of Narasimha also. Apart from this the temple has an awe-inspiring mask of Narasimha which the actor who plays the role of Vishnu's Man-lion incarnation wears every year and it is believed that he enters into a kind of spiritual trance. Thus, the Narasimha drama has a special significance in the Bhagavata Mela dramatic tradition. Many similar dance-drama forms such as Kuchipudi, Therukoothu and Yakshagana are known for their portrayal of Prahlada myth.

However, it is in Orissa that Prahlada Nataka has become a distinct dramatic genre by itself. Only one play is enacted or to be more precise only plays on Narasimha theme are enacted by the troupes of Prahlada Nataka which mostly belong to the Jangam district. It is said that the first

Prahlada Nataka was written by a well-known poet Gopinatha Pariccha but it is ascribed to Raja Ramakrishna Chhotray, the ruler of Jalantar (1857-1905), in whose court the poet flourished. Three more Rajas got three more plays written by their court poets on the same theme and, got them ascribed to themselves.

The Nataka written in folk style without divisions like act or scene is full of songs, interspersed with Sanskrit verses and prose dialogues. There are more than hundred songs and like *Gita Govinda* their ragas and talas are well defined. There are more than twenty characters who appear on the stage in dazzling'and colourful costumes and elaborate make-up.

The Gahaka (or Gayaka—main singer) and his chorus of musicians present the play with their intermittant commentary and explanations of sequences. Each new sequence opens with musical ensemble of harmonium, gini (small brass cymbals) and the Mardala (drum) bringing in added action. Mardala plays significant role in providing rhythm and action to the dancing of important characters. For the vigorous dancing of villain Hiranyakashipu the Mardala particularly weaves intricate patterns of rhythm.

What is most interesting in the Prahlada Nataka is its unusual stage arrangement. A structure with one tier above the other tier, with a wide platform at the top to accomodate the throne of the demon-king is raised in the twenty to thirty square feet area. At some distance is a hallow pillar where Narasimha conseals himself to appear at the appropriate time. The actor playing the role of Narasimha wears a lion mask and sometimes ropes are tied to his waist. The ropes are tied as a precaution to keep the actor under control if he really tries to kill Hiranyakashipu in his frenzy. A boy of eight to twelve years of age generally acts as Prahlada.

Another interesting feature is the use of live animals on the stage. Hiranyakashipu used tp enter the stage mounted on an elephant. Now a dummy elephant is used by the villian who enters mounted on this with pomp and show of fireworks. Live cobras were used to throw around the neck of Prahlada while showing the miracle of his remaining unaffected from serpent-bite. To show the fire-ordeal Prahlada is made to sit on the hub of horizontally placed free-moving wheel and burning torches are fitted to its rim. Then the wheel is given circular momentum. And this gives the appearance as if Prahlada is sitting right in the midst of a ring of fire. The Prahlada Nataka is a spectacular and thrilling entertainment.

Dr. G.N. Mohapatra in his book Jagannatha in History & Religious Traditions of Orissa writes : 'Narasimha cult was popular before the cult of Jagannatha as it is found in Utkala Khanda of Skanda Purana. According to tradition King Indradyumna performed the horse sacrifice and worshipped Narasimha and after that Jagannatha, Balabhadra and subhadra revealed themselves. Then king installed them. Thus the Vaishnavite Narasimha cult has got certain impact on the cult of Vishnu Jagannatha. (p. 355)

The Skanda Purana says that king Indradyumna had a darshan of Bhagavan Narasimha on Nilagiri mountain. He then established a temple of Narasimha in Purushottam Kshetra. In the premises of Jagannatha temple at Puri there is an image of Narasimha.

In the Skanda Purana it is clearly stated that Purushottama Jagannatha was incarnation of Vishnu.

N.P. Joshi in his Bharatitya Murtishastra writes that the oldest Narasimha image, ascribed to pre-Gupta period, is found on a stone slab found at Kondamotu in Andhra Pradesh. Here he is in his full animal form as a lion sitting by the side of Panchaviras. The archaeologists have located about ten Narasimha images belonging to Gupta period. The image at Nachana Kuthara is seen in combat with Hiranyakashipu.

Variety of Narasimha images are found in the Pala art. But most interesting and rare is the image of Lakshmi Narasimha. In a temple in Rajmandir ward of Varanasi there is a six feet high Narasimha image. In upper two hands he is shown holding Ankusha and elephat respectively and lower two arms resting on his legs are in Varada mudra. Deity is seen in sitting padmasana mudra, Lakshmi reclining on his lap.

N.P. Joshi says that in south Narasimha is a popular deity variety of his images having four, six or eight arms can be seen.

Most magnificent monolithic image of Narasimha, ascribed to 15th century A.D., is located at Hampi, capital city of Hindu Empire of Vijayanagara in the south. The hight of the image is eighteen feet and it is 10 feet wide. It is in sitting posture. Varaha was royal insignia of the Empire, but some of the kings who ruled from Hampi were named after Narasimha.

There are certain scriptures related to the cult of Narasimha. Nrisimha Uttara Tapini Upanishad and Nrisimha Purva Tapini Upanishada are connected with Atharva Veda. Also there is one Nrisimhashatchakropanishada. In the 16th century Sankarshana wrote a literary work Nrisimhachampu narrating the story of the deity. In the works like Nrisimhapujapaddhati and Nrisimhaparicharya the method of worshipping Narasimha Bhagavan is discussed. In fourth or fifth century A.D. Narasimha Purana was written to highlight the cult of the deity.

Vamana means dwarf. Vishnu took this incarnation to contain Bali, king of demons, who had gained the kingdom of three worlds and deprived gods of their abode. Jayadeva in his Gita Govinda says :

Wonderous dwarf cleverly deceived Bali,

6

VAMANA

Vamana means dwarf. Vishnu took this incarnation to contain Bali, king of demons, who had gained the kingdom of three worlds and deprived gods of their abode. Jayadeva in his Gita Govinda says :

> Wonderous dwarf cleverly deceived Bali,
> from the nails of his feet flowed water (river Ganga) to make people sanctified,
> O Keshava, assumer of Vamana (dwarf) form Victory to you Jagadisha Hare.

Acharya Nandikeshvara in his Abhinayadarpana suggests the following gesture to indicate Vamana symbolically:

> The four fingers are bent into the palm and the thumb is set on them it is Mushti (fist), when one fist is held upon the other it is Vamana.

The seeds of Vamana incarnation are found in the deeds of Vishnu described in Vedic literature.

The Rig Veda speaks of three steps of Vishnu which he placed in three places. The first two strides were visible but the third led 'beyond the flight of birds' to the abode of gods.

Why according to Rig Vedic sources Vishnu took three steps? In his Vedic Mythology A.A. Macdonell states : 'He thrice traversed the earthly spaces for man in distress. He traversed the earth to bestow it on man for dewelling. He traversed the earthly spaces for wide-stepping existence. With Indra he took vast strides and stretched out the worlds for our existence. (p. 39).

The story in the Shatapatha Brahmana says : 'There arose contention between gods and demons for a place of sacrifice. The latter have stated to have agreed to concede as much land as was equal to the size of dwarf. Vishnu, the dwarf, was then made to lie down. But he grew so big as to encompass the whole earth which consequently passed on to gods. (The Cultural Heritage of India, p. 133).

Epics and Puranas elaborated upon the story and gave it a twist or new versions.

Asura king Bali was grandson of Prahlada, great devotee of Vishnu. He attacked Amaravati, city of Indra in the heaven. The Brahmins of Bhrugu clan had made him very powerful who performed a Yajna named Vishvajeet for him. Seeing that Virochanaputra Bali had become very powerful the gods headed by Indra quietly left their abode and ran away. After capturing Amaravati he conquered all the three worlds.

The Bhrugu brahmins made Bali perform one hundred Ashvamedha Yajnas and his fame spread in all directions.

This made Devamata Aditi very depressed and sad. She expressed her sorrow before her husband Maharshi Kashyapa and requested him to do something to restore the lost glory of her sons, the gods.

Maharshi Kashyapa asked her to observe Payovrata to please Vishnu. Pleased by her penance Lord Vishnu himself appeared before her and assured her that he would be born as her son and restore all the glories of gods. One day when moon was on Shravana Nakshatra. The tithi was dwadashi with Sravan Nakshatra of Shuklapaksha of Bhadrapada Masa which was also known asVijaya dwadashi. The sun was stationed in the centre of the sky. The Lord Vishnu appeared as a son of Aditi. Immediately he assumed the form of Dwarf Brahmachari Vamana batu, as actor swiftly changes his appearance.

On the bank of river Narmada there is a very beautiful place called Bhrigukaccha. There the Ritwija of Brugu clan were performing Yajna for Bali. One day they saw a Vamana Batu coming towards the Yajna mandapa. He was shining like a sun. In his hands he was holding umbrella (chatra), stick (danda and pot filled with water (kamandalu). When he entered the Yajna Mandapa where Ashvameda was being performed, everybody stood and welcomed him. All his limbs were tiny and beautiful. Bali requested him to ask for anything he desired and he would give it to him.

Vamana asked him to give him a bit of earth, equal in measure to three tiny steps of his feet. When Bali lifted the Jalapatra to pour water on the hands of Vamana indicating that he had granted him his wish.

Daityaguru Shukracharya understood everything. He told Bali that the dwarf was none else but Bhagavan Vishnu himself. He is Vishvarupa and in just three strides he would cover all the three worlds and deprive you of everything you possess.

But Bali did not listen to him. He took water in his hand and vowed to give Vamana land measuring his three small strides.

Then and there a miracle happened. Vamana form of Ananta Bhagavan started growing and occupied entire universe. All the Asuras were frightened to see the Vishvarupa of Vaman Bhagavan. Soon his terrible weapons appeared on the scene which he held in his hands. He covered entire earth, Prithvi, by his one feet, his body measured the sky and all directions, by his second stride he covered entire heaven, Swarga.

Understanding the desire of Vishnu his bird vehicle Garuda tied Bali with Varuna-pasha. Smiling at him Vamana said to Bali that still he had to grant him the space to take the third stride.

Bali humbly requested Vamana in his Vishvarupa form to place his third step on his head.

Vamanarupa Vishnu asked Bali to go and live in Sutala along with his Asura army. Bali obeyed him and since then he is residing in Sutala region.

Suvira Jaiswal thinks that the tale perhaps hints at supression of a cult of Bali, for Varahamihira (author of Brihatsamhita, 6th century A.D.) gives instructions for making a cult image of Bali, and it seems that demon-king also received some kind of worship. The Junagadi inscription of Skandagupta begins with the invocation to the Dwarf incarnation of Vishnu.

The cult of Bali could have been a possibility as a grand festival of Onam is celebrated in Kerala in his honour. According to legend Bali was ruler of the ancient land of Kerala. He was most benevolent king in his reign his subjects enjoyed prosperity and peace. Before leaving earth under the threat of Vamana and going to neither region he sought his permission to visit his subjects once in a year which was granted to him. The people of Kerala celebrate the arrival of their king to meet them on Thiruvonam day in the Malayalam month of Chingam (August-September).

The image of Vamana, shown as placing his raised foot on the head of Bali to push him down to nether world, is worshipped in the famous temple of Tiruvellikkara. In the houses clay images of Vamana are installed and worshipped.

The second day of the festival is considered as most important because it is the day of visit of king Bali. Floral decorations are made to welcome him, every home is kept bright and shining, sumptuous feasts and entertainments in the form of various types of games and sports are arranged, but most spectacular is the snake boat races which are held at many places. At Trichur great elephant procession is taken out amidst spectacular fire works. At Shornur colourful Kathakali plays are enacted.

N.P. Joshi writes that since Gupta period we start getting the Vamana images mostly in his Trivikrama form, meaning one raised foot kept on the head of Bali. A beautiful image of Dwarf Vamana is housed in the Ashutosha Museum, Calcutta. It is ascribed to 11th century A.D.

A Purana work named Vamana Purana was written around seventh century A.D. It is believed that it was written in Kurukshetra region. The opening verse of this Purana is dedicated to Vamana incarnation of Vishnu.

7

PARASHURAMA

Parashurama represents that part of history bloodied by severe caste wars, revenge being its main theme. He was expert in weaponary of all kinds but his main weapon being Parashu, axe, he became famous as Parashu-ram. About him Jayadeva in his "Dashvatara Ashtapadi says :

You washed evil from the world
in a flood of warrior's blood

And pain of existence is eased

You take the form of Bhrugupati

O Keshava assumer of Axeman Priest form,
Victory to you Jagadisha Hare

Acharya Nandikeshvara in his Abhinaya Darpana tells us how to represent Parashurama by hand gestures. He says :

Left hand on hips and right in Ardha Patak. A little finger of Tripatak is also bent in Ardha Patak.

Parashuram story essentially found in the epic Mahabharatat's Vanaparva.

Once upon a time king Kartavirya Arjan of Kshatriya Haihaya race was ruling over the earth. By the grace of Lord Dattatreya he got a golden flying machine which he used to roam about. He had thousands arms. Astride his chariot he would move around the world troubling Yakshas and Rishis and whosoever came in his way. Once he attacked king of gods who was sporting with his wife, Shachi. This led Vishnu to think about destroying him.

That time there was a country on the earth named Kanyakubja which was ruled by a powerful king by name Gadhi. Leaving his capital he started living in forest. During his sojourn in the forest his wife gave birth to a beautiful daughter.

Brahmarshi Richik asked for her hand in marriage, King Gadhi told him that according to the custom prevalent in his community he would be required to give him one thousand horses having black ears to the king as a shulka, price, for the bride.

Richik went to Lord Varuna who gave him one thousand horses with black ears known as Shyamakarna. Accepting the bride-price king Gadhi gave his daughter Satyavati to Richik in Kanyakubja city on the bank of river Ganga.

They had a son by name Jamadagni who left other Rishis far behind in the knowledge of Vedas and acquired the knowledge of archery and other weapons. Jamadagni went to king Prasenjit and asked for her daughter Renuka to become his wife. The couple had five sons, the fifth being Parashuram.

One day Renuka went to river for taking bath. There she saw king Chitraratha who was by wearing the garland of lotus flowers, amorously sporting in the river water. Infatuated by what she saw Renuka too desired the company of Chitraratha.

Jamadagni by his spiritual powers understood the state of mind of his wife. Angered by this sacrilage he one by one ordered his sons to behead her. Stunned by the words of their father his four sons simply stood motionless. Cursing them the Rishi ordered his fifth son to do the task. Without thinking for a moment he did what his father asked him to do.

Pleased by the obdience of Parashurama Rishi asked him to seek any boon he desired. Parashurama asked him to bring back to life his mother Renuka. The crisis was over.

One day king Kartavirya Arjun, ruler of Anupa country, during his wanderings came across the hermitage of Rishi Jamadagni. His wife Renuka welcomed him but arrogant king destroyed the hermitage and took away the calf of Homadhenu. On his way he destroyed big trees around the hermitage. When Parashurama came to know about this he lifted his bow and arrows and started persuing the king. After locating him Parashurama attacked him, cut his thousand arms and left him to die.

When sons of Kartavirya Arjun came to know about the death of their father they attacked the hermitage of Jamadagni and killed him mercilessly. Angered by this Parashurama pledged to destroy entire Kshatriya, warrior, clan. He killed all the sons of Kartavirya Arjuna and eliminated all the Kshatriyas from the surface of earth, not once but twentyone times. He filled five wells with their blood situated in Samantapanchak kshetra.

He donated all the land own from Kshatriyas to Maharshi Kashyapa and went to Mahendra Parvat to live there.

The conflict between Haihaya Kshatriyas and Bhrugu Brahmins was variously explained by the scholars as they saw in it a fact of history.

Brahmins and Kshatriyas had certain relationship in the past. Brahmins were advisors, counselors of the Kshatriya kings and as such enjoyed certain status and previlages. Haihayas tried to destroy this equation by their rash acts and paid for it. The crisis grew into Kshatriya Brahmin conflict of great magnitude, ultimately harming both the sides.

Alain Danielou in his Hindu Polytheism writes : 'Parasu-Rama is said to have defeated and destroyed the chivalrous aristocracy which thought itself the master of mankind, he re-established the principle of a monarchy controlled by a priestly class. Another interpretation is this that it represents the final defeat of the non-Aryan kingdoms and of their kings, who had been invested with priestly functions by the Aryan theocracy. Parasu-Rama's hostility to Kshatriyas evidently indicates a severe struggle between them and the Brahmanas for supremacy.

The scene of Parasu-Rama's exploits is said to have been the south-west coast of India (though some of the Puranas place it near the river Narmada) whose non-brahmin inhabitants still claim to be decendents of Kshatriyas defeated by Parashurama.' (p. 171).

Mahabharata says that due to Parashurama's actions there prevailed anarchy on the earth. Kshyapa Rishi asked Parashurama to go and live on the western part of southern sea-shore. He then went around and found out Kshatriyas who were in hiding. He then made them kings and established the political order on the earth.

Parashurama reclaimed land from the sea from Brigukaccha to Kanyakumari for himself. This region came to be known as Parashurama Kshetra or Shurparaka country. Brahmanda Purana has different legend to tell about how Parashurama reclaimed this land from sea. It was to settle the Brahmins of Mahabaleshvar-Gokarna region as they faced submersion from ocean, due to excavation done by the sons of Sagara in Ganga basin.

There are number of stories about Parashurama in the Mahabharata. One relates to Karna.

Karna was a great warrior of Suta caste. He keenly desired to learn the archery to perfection and know the technique indomitable Brahmastra. He went to Parashurama who was staying on Mahendra mountain. Karna introduced himself as Bhruguvamshi Brahmin to Parashurama. Pleased by his behaviour Parashurama accepted him as his disciple and started giving him lessons in archery.

Karna won the confidence of his teacher who taught him how to use terrible Brahmastra.

One day feeling tired Parashurama lied down to rest with his head on the lap of his disciple. Suddenly an insect named Alarka started digging a hole in the thigh of Karna. Despite of great pain he was suffering on account of an insect drilling hole in his thigh Karna did not budge from his position, fearing that may disturb the sleep of his teacher.

Parashuram woke up with a start when the blood oozing out of Karna's wound touched his body.

Angry Parashurama asked Karna as to who he was. He said no Brahmin could tolerate such a pain and he seemed to had tolerance of a Kshatriya. Afraid of Guru's anger Karna revealed his real identity. Parashurama said : O fool you deceived me by telling lies..Your knowledge of Brahmastra will remain with you till you face adversary of equal skill and bravery in the battlefield and when your death will be near.

Karna argued that the Guru who teaches Vedas and Vidya was just like a father. By this logic Parashurama too became his father. Hence he declared himself to be of his Bhargava Brahmin Gotra.

This glib talk of Karna infuriated Parashurama still more. He told him that unless a person is Brahmin the Brahmastra could never be with him. Taking pity on hapless Karna Parashurama told him that still being his disciple no Kshatriya on the earth would be able to compete with him on the battlefield.

Ramayana describes the conflict between Dasharathi Rama and Bhargava Parashurama, a Kshatriya and Brahmin, ending the supremacy of the later.

The epic says that after breaking mighty bow of Shiva, Shiva Dhanusya, Rama, son of Dasharatha, married Sita, daughter of Janaka, king of Videha. After marriage ceremony as Rama was proceeding to his capital city of Ayodhya, suddenly Parashurama appeared before him.

Everybody was frightened to see the angry axe wielding Brahmin with a bow in his hand.

He appreciated Rama for his act of breaking the mighty bow of Shiva and said that it really was a wonderful act of strength and bravery. However, he told him, to prove himself how he should pick up the one he was carrying which was a Vaishnava bow of Vishnu and place an arrow on it.

Rama accepted the challenge. He quite easily took the bow from Bhrugu Nandan and placed an arrow on it.

Rama told Parashurama that he did not want to shoot the arrow at him but he would certainly destroy his power to move anywhere he desired and various divine abodes he had earned by the merit of his penance.

Parashurama requested him to destroy the fruits of his merit but allow him to retain his power to move around as willed.

Rama did exactly that and crestfallen Parashurama returned to his hermitage on the mountain Mahendra. Before his departure he told Rama that he was not feeling sorry for his defeat because he suffered it at the hands of Trilokinatha Hari himself, as Rama was none but his incarnation.

Dasharathanandana Sri Rama offered worship to great warrior Bhrugupati Parashurama with due respect. Parashurama then left for Mahendra Parvata.

This was virtually the end of Parashurama incarnation though he lived even after that being one of the eight legandary immortal souls.

N.P. Joshi in his Bharatiya Murtishastra writes that it is very rarely we get the independant image of Parashurama. His image of Gupta period was found near Gwalior. In the village Timba in Gujarat similar Parashurama image of the same period was recovered reports D. Kalpana Desai.

A temple of Parashurama is located at city of Chiploon in Konkan region of Maharashtra. Another in near Simla.

There are certain places of Pilgrimage associated with the name of Parashurama. In the north India near Meerut city there is a place called Panchatirthi which is a confluence of five rivers. It is believed that the hermitage of Jamadagni was at this place. It was here, the legend says, Parashurama was born and killed Sahasrarjuna. Here is a Shiva temple named Parashurameshvara.

Western Ghat in Maharashtra is identified as Mahendra Parvat, the abode of Parashurama. At the mouth of river Narmada there is a village named Loharya. It is believed that Parashurama performed penance here. Near Simla there is a place called Renuka tirtha.The sacred tank here is named as Parashuram tal. The mountain here is known as Jamadagni Parvat. Here are temples of Renuka and Parashurama.

After donating entire earth won by him Parashurama went to a place named Shurparaka. It is identified as village Sopara near Mumbai, Maharashtra. On the border of Kurukshetra there is a place called Samantapanchak. According to Mahabharata here Parashurama created five waterbodies, kundas. This place is now famous as Ramahrida.

Padma Purana after narrating the story of Parashurama says that devotees should worship only Rama and Krishna because they were full incarnations. Parashurama was merely a part incarnation who possessed divine energy only for some time, temporarily.

However on the day of Vaishakha shuddha tritiya or Akshaya tritiya the festival of Parashurama Jayanti is celebrated in south India. A Tantric work parashuramkalpasutra and another scripture Parashurama Pratap are read by his devotees.

The cult of mother goddess Renuka, mother of Parashurama, is very popular in Maharashtra and Karnataka in particular. She is known by different names such as Yellamma, Yamai, Ekavira. Originally a Dravidian folk deity. According to Lilacharitra, 13th century work in Marathi, she, at time, was offered the oblation of liquor and meat. In a work known as Renuka Mahatmya many myths associated with her origin are given.

It is belived that Mahur in Maharashtra is her main station. It was here, according to local legend, Parashurama performed last rites of his father Jamadagni and Renuka committed Sati.

At Mahur her Tanḍala or image showing her face only is worshipped but according to some scholars she is worshipped in the form of Lajjagauri. It is believed that Renuka is pre-Dravidian earth-mother goddess. The Parashurama-Jamadagni- Renuka myth was later addition to her original mythology.

Devotees of Renuka like Gondhali, Jogati-Jogatini, Bhutye are kind of folk priests who sing and perform the songs of the deity.

8

RAMA

Dasharathi Rama, prince of Ayodhya, an epic hero and most probably a historical person was accored the status of being an incarnation of Vishnu much later than the publication of his biography, the Ramayana, by Valmiki. In the original Ramayana itself there is no mention of his being one. Even after attaing divine stature it took couple of centuries for Rama cult to pick up.

Jayadeva in his Dashavatara Ashtapadi in Gita Govinda describing Rama incarnation says :

You paid the homage to ten Dikpalas
by the Bali of ten heads of Ravana
O Keshava, assumer of the form of Rama
Victory to you Jagadisha Hare.

Acharya Nandikeshvara in his Abhinaya Darpana describing the symbolic hand gesture of Rama says :

> Left hand in Kapittha mudra and right in Shikhara Mudra. If the thumb of the Mushti (fist) is raised it is Shikhara. The forefinger of Shikhara is bent over top of the thumb is Kapittha - Elephat apple.

Story of the Ramayana is not found in the Vedic literature nor it's hero's name. But certainly Sita, the heroine of the epic is borrowed from Vedic literature. Sita as 'furrow as in a ploughed field' is mentioned in the Rig Veda (4.57, 6-7) with veneration and worship is offered to her with the prayer that she should bring the abundant produce. In later works she was personified as goddess of fertility. In the Paraskara Sutra she is described as 'wife of Indra'.

Sita too was, according to Ramayana, found covered with mud when king Janaka was ploughing a field for sacrifice.

Generally her role in the epic as dutiful wife is stressed. Cornelia Dimmitt in her article Sita in the book. The Divine Consort says :

'A deeper study of Sita in the Ramayana yields another picture of her from that of dutiful wife. She can be seen to display the qualities of the goddess in two different modes; as mistress of the plants and animals she is immediately related to the fertility of the earth and as Shakti, the energy that inspires the hero Rama to action, she is the source of his power as king.' (p. 216).

Many centuries earlier, to be precise in 16th century, Marathi saint Ekanatha wrote a work called Adhyatma Ramayana. The first book of it comprises what is called Ramahridaya, which was narrated to Hanumat by Sita, who says that as the original Prakriti, she does everything and did all deeds mentioned in the Ramayana, while Rama as a only existing soul is inactive, unchangeable and blessed, and is a mere witness to her deeds.' Vaishnavism, Saivism and Minor Religious Systems. (p. 48).

While creating the character of Rama, somewhere at the back of his mind he held the concept of Vedic Indra, great warrior god. The battle Rama fought with demon king Ravana is likened to Indra-Vritra fight. However Rama as a hero is not the copy of Vedic Indra, both have their independent personalities and mythologies. Rama story has no Vedic roots.

From floating mass of Rama literature in the form of Gathas, ancient Itihasa-Purana works and Akhyana literature Valmiki weaved his own enchanting epic in Sanskrit which became famous as Ramayana. Ayana means treatise as well as advancing, procession, path, course. Ramayana describes the course of Rama's life, path he charted from North to South, his advance from Ayodhya to Lanka of the Yatra of his life.

Some scholars feel that the epic poetry developed from the literary genre of Vedic period known as Gatha Narasamshi, praise songs of men. Maurice Winternitz in his History of Indian Literature, Vol. 1 says : 'In addition to Itihasas and Puranas also the Gatha Narasamshi, praise song of men, are mentioned (Shatapatha Brahmana XI, 5, 6,8; Ashvalayana Grihyas. III. 3) and these we may consider to be the actual fore-runners of a hero-epic.' (p. 293).

In the Yajna the ballad singer with lute used to be invited to sing in the praise of the sacrificer saying this battle he fought and won and that foe he conquered, etc. Such traditions might have given birth to epic works.

Well before Valmiki composed his epic the Gathas depicting Rama stories were popular in the masses. Harivamsha Purana, considered to be an appendix of Mahabharata, speaks of Gathas about Rama which the knower of Puranic lore used to sing (41.149).

There was a great tradition of Gatha singers since ancient times. From Rig Veda we come to know that the singers of the Gathas were known as Gathin (1. 7. 1). The best among them were recognised as Riju-Gatha (5445). In the Ashtadhyayi of Panini male and female singers of Gathas were termed as Gathaka and Gathika respectively (111.1.146). We already know of composing and singing of Gathas on sacrifice performing king in Vedic times. Rama as a king, says Ramayana, performed Yajnas. May be Gathas composed at that time were preserved by Ikshvaku dynasty kings following him. In the Balakanda of Ramayana it is said that in the royal family of Ikshvaku's a Akhyana came down by tradition which became famous as Ramayana.

One of the oldest versions of Rama story is found in the collection of Jataka stories which is the part of Buddhist

Tripitaka literature. The title of the Jataka referred to above is Dasharatha Jataka (No. 461) It. says :

> In ancient times there lived in Varanasi a king named Dasharatha. Out of his sixteen thousand wives the eldest gave birth to three children named Rama Pandit, Lakhan Kumar and Sita Devi. After her death king Dasharatha made another wife his chief queen. In due course she gave birth to a son, Bharata. Pleased king gave her his blessings which implied that he promised her to fulfill any one of her desires.

When Bharat Kumar attained the age of eight years, the chief queen reminding the king of his blessings said that the kingdom should be given to her son, Bharata. King Dasharata called his other children and asked them to leave the capital and go to forest least their step mother would not hesitage to kill them.

Rama Pandit, Lakhan Kumar and their sister Sita went in exile and started living in Himalayas. Nine years passed and king died of sorrow.

Bharat went to Himalayas to bring back his brothers and sister to hand over the reigns of kingdom to them. When Bharata informed Rama about the death of their father he remained unmoved. But when Rama Pandit conveyed this sad news to Lakhan Kumar and Sita, unable to bear the sorrow of their father's death, they became unconscious.

Surprised Bharata asked Rama Pandit that how he remained free of sorrow. In reply Rama Pandit recited ten Gathas describing inevitability of death and futility of feeling sad about it. Bharat requested Rama Pandit to return to Varanasi and become the king. But Rama refused his offer saying that he would return only after completing twelve years of his exile.

After completing twelve years Rama returned to Varanasi with Lakhan Kumar and Sita. Rama was coronated along with Sita. And they ruled for sixteen thousand years thereafter.

The Jataka informs that Rama Pandita was none else but Bodhisatva himself and the whole story was narrated to underline the futility of feeling disturbed over the death of near and dear one including father.

The Jataka is made up of verses (Gathas) and prose portion. Some scholars think that the verses belonged to great antiquity (sixth-fifth century B.C.) and prose portion was comparitively recent. Some scholars think that prose and verse portions existed together, as it was impossible to understand the Jataka unless they are together.

It is also believed that along with the decline of Buddhism in India its literature too was lost to posterity. However it was preserved in the monasteries in Lanka. Around fifth century A.D. these works were translated into Pali and brought back to India. In the process the Gathas remained true to the original but prose portion was recreated later on, that is in fifth century A.D.

But considering only the Gathas we find startling similarities between Gathas in Dasharata Jataka and Valmiki's Ramayana as brought out by Bhadanta Anand Kausalyanana (Jataka, Prathama Khanda, p. 24). Either both had borrowed from the same source or Ramayana took them from Buddhist Jatakas which were composed much earlier, about 6th century B.C. Dasharatha Jataka is found sculpted at Bharhut Stupa railings and later at Buddhist monument of Nagarjunakonda.

The Rishyasringa story's earlier version Nalinika Jataka is found in collection of Jataka tales. It's depiction is found on a railing pillar housed in Mathura Museum datable to third century A.D.

In the Buddhist Sama Jataka there is a story of king inadvertly shooting a hermit boy mistaking him as a beast who had come to drink water of river. In fact the boy had been to river to fetch water for his blind perents.

In the Ramayana the same story is told with Dasharatha, father of Rama, as a central figure. The story of Jataka is painted on the wall of cave No 10 of Ajantha.

There are a few more Gathas in Jataka tales which exhibits the knowledge of Rama story. A Gatha in the Jayaddisa Jataka says : 'As Rama's mother wished him well when he went to Dandaka forest, I am also wishing you well.'

Incidently Dasharatha Jataka do not mention Dandaka forest. In the Mahavessantara Jataka there is an interesting Gatha which says : 'I am the wife of a prince in exile. I do not neglect him as Sita never neglect Rama.'

However in the fifth century A.D. in his work Digha Nikaya Attakatha Acharya Buddhaghosha says that Akhyana means Bharata and Ramayana and one should never venture near the place where they were being recited. He further says that the stories about Bharata war and kidnapping of Sita are simply meaningless – niratthaka katha.

Bhadanta Anand Kausalyayana feels that the earlier versions of Rama and Pandava stories are found in the Buddhist literature. The Ramayana and the Mahabharata are more elaborate, ornate and inflated form of these earlier versions (Jataka, Prathama Khanda, p. 25-26).

There is a strong literary tradition of Jain Ramayanas starting from Pauma-cariya of Vimala Suri written sometimes in the end of third or at the beginning of fourth century A.D. According to vimala Suri,the story of Rama was first narrated by Lord Mahavira to his disciples and it came down to him. He says that Rama story tradition of Jainas is different from found in Valmiki Ramayana.

He further states that he was making all efforts to remove the absurdities that had crept in the Valmiki Ramayana to make the story more rational. However scholars like V.M. Kulkarni had come to the conclusion that 'except for the number of queens of Rama and Lakshmana, and killing of Ravana by Lakshmana and Jainistic conclusion, his story of Rama is basically same as found in the Hindu version of Valmiki.'

About Jainistic conclusion V.M. Kulkami states : 'After Lakshmana's death Rama became a monk, practised austerities, obtained perfect knowledge, and in due course ottained moksha (final liberation). Lakshmana, as he did not accept the path laid down by Jinas, sank into hell. Ravana too, for his lapse from the code of correct behaviour, had to go to hell. It was laid down that both of them after passing through many births would attain liberation. Sita, after living the life of Aryika was reborn in heaven, she too in course of time obtain moksha.' (The Ramayana Tradition in Asia, p. 226-241).

Jataka Rama story is pre-Ramayana (of Valmiki) in origin but all the Jain Ramakathas were written much after it and carried the influence of Valmiki's work. Both the religions trace the Rama story to their founders, Buddha and Mahavira. Jain tradition says that originally Ram Katha was narrated by Mahavira. Buddhist go a step further and say that Rama was none but incarnation of Bodhisattva. However Valmiki's version of Rama story is considered as definitive work which gained immense popularity. Based on it many versions came into being in number of languages in India and abroad.

There is lot of controversy as to when Valmiki composed his Ramayana. Generally it is ascribed to the period around 5th century B.C.

It is believed that the original text of Valmiki underwent expansion from time to time with the addition of extraneous material till fourth century A.D. Most significant additions were Ayodhya Kanda and Uttara Kanda which were composed sometimes in the early centuries of Christian era, according to some in the second century A.D. It was in these two added chapters Rama was declared as an incarnation of Vishnu. From that time divinity of Rama was established, we find his name included in the list of Vishnu's avataras in the Mahabharata and several other Puranas. Kalidasa in his Raghuvamsha, ascribed to 4th-5th century A.D. counts Ram among incarnation of Vishnu.

Gradually the popularity of Ramayana started growing. We find elaborate description of dramatisation of Ramayana in Harivamsha Purana composed around 3rd-4th century A.D. Buddhists were not very happy about the popularity of the epics. C.D. Godakumbura in his article in the Ramayana in Srilanka in the book The Ramayana Tradition in Asia write:

'Papancasudant, the Pali commentary on 'the Majjhima Nikaya (of the fifth century A.D.), classes narratives such as the story of the Bharata war and tale of the abduction of Sita as frivolous and useless talk (Bharatayuddha-Sitaharanadiniratthakatha purekkharata tatharupikathaka-thanamca—op. cit. PTS ed pt 1, p. 201). This was reechoed and elaborated upon by Sinhelese writers. The preacher monk, Dharmasena, the contemporary of the writer of the above cited portions of the Culavamsa who was slightly earlier, in his book of Buddhist stories, the Sadharma-ratnavaliya (Jayatilak a ed p. 952), while speaking of the recital of the epics in North Indian kingdoms and cities, – a list of which he gives, – says that the people of those countries paid gold, bullion and coins, and got the stories such as those of Rama and Sita which are hinderance to the attainment of heaven.' (p. 436).

This means that Buddhist stories were gradually losing their popularity compared to Hindu epics around 5th century A.D.

Banabhatta, in his prose masterpiece Kadambari written in 7th century A.D. states that the citizens of Ujjayani were lovers of Mahabharata, Purana and Ramayana (Mahabharata -purana-ramananuragina) and they where as chivalrous to women as Lakshmana was and Loved Bharata's Natyashastra as Shatrughna loved brother Bharata.

Rama is known to South India as epic hero and incarnation of Vishnu minos early days. He is found mentioned in Tamil Sangam Literature ascribed to first two centuries of Christian era. In post Sangam epics in Tamil Silapaddhikaram and Manimekhalai contain references to Rama. The most famous Tamil Ramayana version is poet Kamban's Ramavatara Mahakatha in 9th century A.D. Vaishnavite Alvars and Shaivite Nayanmars who spear—headed Bhakti movement in South in 7th and 8th centuries A.D. made Ramakatha popular by writing poetic composition. Exquisite Chola bronze images of Rama, Lakshmana, Sita and Hanumana attest to the popularity of Ramakatha.

Once Maharshi Valmiki asked divine sage Narada as to who was the most ideal person living on the earth. To this Narada in his reply said that it was none else but Rama, prince of Ayodhya, belonging to Ikshvaku dynasty.

After Narada left Maharshi, emersed in deep thought, walked down towards river Tamasa and started moving in the dense forest on her bank. He then saw a pair of Krauncha birds moving around joyfully enjoying each others company. Suddenly a Nishada, hunter by profession, appeared on the scene and hit the male bird of the pair with his arrow. Seeing his female companion crying pathetically, the heart of compassionate sage was filled with deep pathos and sorrow. Moved by emotions that swelled in his heart the sage pronounced a curse in a verse form.

He said : 'You, O hunter, killed one of the Krauncha birds whose heart was set upon making love to his consort. As a consequence, hence forth, your mind will know no peace.'

Suddenly Maharshi realised that in fact, moved by emotions he had made a poetic statement in a shloka metre which has a potential to be sung on the accompaniment of Tantri, a stringed musical instrument.

Maharshi took a ritual bath in the river and brooding over the incident he returned to his hermitage. In a rare moment of sudden inspiration the shoka (sorrow) became shloka (a poetic metre). When Maharshi was contemplating on this Lord Brahma arrived in his hermitage. He advised Maharshi to use the same poetic metre to describe the life story of Rama, prince of Ayodhya and thus the epic Ramayana was born. Maharshi taught his young disciples, Lava and Kusha, how to sing it and after learning it they started singing it in their beautiful voice wherever they went.

It is interesting to note that in the Chaturtha Sarga of the Balakanda the Ramayana is described as 'Great life-story of Sita', Sitayascharitam Mahat, whose other title was Paulastya Vadham or Vanquishing of Ravana.

To say that Ramayana was the biography of Sita and it's central theme was killing of Ravana. Indeed the Rama-Ravana war was not only fought over Sita but due to her insistance also.

In the 37th sarga of the Sunder Kanda when Hanumana who tracked her down to Ashoka Vana in the island of Lanka, offered to carry her back on his back to her husband, she refused. She told him that Rama being Kshatriya, it will be proper for him to come to Lanka himself, kill the ten-headed monster, Ravana, and rescue her honarably. She meant that her honour must be avanged through war.

Another inference we can draw from the other title of the epic, Paulastya Vadha, that the epic in its original form must have been ending with the killing of Ravana.

Now let us relate the story of Rama as depicted in Valmiki Ramayana chapter by chapter.

BAL KANDA

Dasharatha was the king of Ikshvaku dynasty ruling over prosperous Koshala Janapada on the bank of river Sarayu with the city of Ayodya as its capital. He had three wives but no sons. For begetting sons he performed a Yajna ritual with Rishyasringa as chief priest. By the blessings of

Vishnu he got four sons – Rama, Bharat, Lakshman and Shatrughna.

One day sage Vishvamitra came to Dasharatha and asked him to send his son, Rama, to protect the rituals they were performing in his hermitage. Rama and his brother Lakshmana accompanied Vishvamitra and ably protected the ritual sacrifices killing demons Maricha and Subahu and hoards of demons accompaning them.

But before that, as they were proceeding towards hermitage, they killed Yakshi turned demoness Tataka who possessed magical occult powers and capacity to fly in the sky ruling over a forest known as Tataka Vana. She was a cannibal by nature and had inhuman strength of one thousand elephants.

Pleased Vishvamitra gave them two Vidyas, Bala and Atibala and taught them how to handle powerful weapons, known as Divyastras.

After killing the demons plaguing the hermitage of Vishvamitra the brothers Rama and Lakshmana proceeded towards the city of Mithila to attend the Yajna being performed by king Janaka. On the way Vishvamitra told him many interesting stories.

In the suberb of Mithila there was a deserted hermitage. Once upon a time it belonged to sage Gautama. His wife Ahalya was very beautiful and even king of gods, Indra, desired her. One day Indra assuming the form of Gautama approached her. Ahalya recognised him but submitted to his request of making love, curious to know the skills of Devaraj Indra. Both were satisfied by making love to each other. But when sage Gautama came to know about this he cursed both.

On reaching the deserted hermitage Rama saw Ahalya. When Ahalya saw Rama her curse ended and she united with her husband, sage Gautama.

After reaching Mithila Rama broke the mighty bow of

Shiva in the possession of king Janaka and married his daughter Sita. His other brothers too got beautiful brides.

On his way back to Ayodhya Parashurama angered by the news of Rama breaking the Shiva's bow stopped Rama. But Rama defeated him, after which Parashurama left for Mahendra mountain, his abode.

This kanda is full of legends, stories, myths narrated by Vishvamitra. The material of Buddhist Nalinika Jataka and Sama Jataka are found weaved in Dasharatha's life story. A story from Yakshi cult, which finds mention in Buddhist Jatakas and later in Brihat Katha, is added in the form of the tale of Tataka.

Importantly here Rama is described as an incarnation of Vishnu. It is believed that this Kanda was added to original Ramayana much later.

AYODHYA KANDA

In the beginning we are told that prince Bharata along with brother Shatrughna had gone to the city of Rajgriha in Kekaya country which happened to be Matrukula of Bharata. Behind their back Dasharata decided to make Rama heir of his throne. It was a clever political move to weedout possible opposition if any from brother Bharata. However, Dashratha's young and beautiful wife Kaikeyi opposed the move and staked the claim of her son Bharata. Kaikeyi compelled the king to send Rama in exile in forest for twelve years and declare Bharata as crown prince.

Rama left Ayodhya with wife Sita and brother Lakshmana for Chitrakuta forest. Dashratha died of grief. Bharata was called back to Ayodhya. Angry Bharata severely rebuked mother Kikeyi for her greed.

He then proceeded to meet Rama and camped at the hermitage of Bharadwaja Rishi along with his army. From there he went to meet Rama at Chitrakuta. Rama refused to return to Ayodhya before completing twelve years of exile. Taking respectfully the charana-paduka, foot wear, of Rama,

Bharata returned to Nandigrama and keeping those on the throne, he started looking after the affairs of the state in the name of his elder brother.

Rama leaving the Chitrakuta moved to the hermitage of Atri Rishi, from there he proceeded to enter dense forest of Dandakaranya.

In this Kanda there is a chapter describing dionysian orgy indulged in by the soldiers of Bharata in the hermitage of Bharadwaja Rishi which looks out of place. It is generally believed that only in the first and concluding last Kandas of the epic Rama is described as an incarnation of Vishnu but in the Prathama Sarge of Ayodhyakanda (verse 7) it is said that Rama was Sanatana Vishnu himself who took incarnation in Manushya Loka with the intention of killing Ravana in response to the prayers of gods. Probably this verse too might have been later interpolation.

ARANYA KANDA

This Kanda tells us how Rama came into conflict with forest-dwelling community, probably of tribals opposing the Yajna culture progressively making inroads in their region and termed as Rakshasas which simply meant demons.

When in the midst of Dandaka forest they saw a huge demon named Viradha. When Viradha attacked them he got killed by Rama and his brother and burried him deep in the earth as was the custom of Rakshasa clan.

Sita tried to persuade Rama from killing Rakshas. She was against Rama and Lakshmana entering forest of Dandaka with weapons in their hands. The weapons may inspire them to kill the Rakshasa, she told them. She told Rama not to kill the Rakshasas living in Dandaka forest as they were not his enemies. She implored him to follow Dharma which teaches non-violence, particularly during the stay in Tapovana a place to perform religious austerities. Rama refused to listen to her advise on the pretext that he had already committed to protect Yajna—performing Brahmins and Rishis by killing the demons.

During their wanderings Maharshi Agastya advised them to built a hermitage for their stay at Panchavati on the bank of river Godavari.

On his way to Panchavati Rama met a huge bird named Jatayu who was friend of his father.

Lakshmana built a beautiful hermitage made up of huts made out of grass and dried leaves, or Parnashalas, and they all started living there. One day demoness Shurpanakha, sister of Ravana, the king of Lanka, saw Rama and was infatuated by the handsome prince. She approached Rama and requested him to be her husband. She boastfully told him that Ravana was son of Vishrava Muni and her other brothers were Mahabali Kumbhakarna and Vibhishana. About Vibhishana, she told him that he was a person of religious bent of mind, Dharmatma, and hardly adehers to Rakshasa ways of life. She told him that they were living in the Rakshasa country which was protected by her other two brothers Khara and Dushana.

Rama laughed loudly and told her that as he was a married person with wife by his side she may approach Lakshmana. Lakshmana cleverly persuaded her to go to Rama instead. She returned to Rama and told him that if the woman with you was the only hinderence in their union she would kill her by eating her alive.

With these worlds she ferociously attacked Sita. Addressing the Rakshasas as Anaryas who indulge in cruel actions not worth making fun of Rama asked Lakshmana to deface her. Lakshmana cut her nose and ears.

Crying with pain she entered the forest and told Khara, her brother her story of defacement. Khara who was surrounded by Rakshasa sent the army of fourteen thousand demons to kill Rama who had intruded in their land with his brother and wife. Led by Shurpanakha the demons attacked Rama who vanquished them all.

Shurpanakha again went back to brother Khara. Rama killed him, his brother Dushana, along with their huge army.

Janasthana where Rama was living was territory under Ravana's control. A demon named Akampana rushed to Lanka to tell king Ravana about the terrible killings of his followers. Shurpanakha too reached Lanka and advised him to kidnap beautiful wife of Rama as an act of revenge.

One day Sita saw a beautiful golden deer. She requested Rama to catch it for her. Entrusting the task of protecting her Rama went to hunt it. Sita sends away Lakshmana too to help Rama. Ravana meanwhile in the guise of an ascetic kidnapped Sita. Bird Jatayu intervened but was killed by Ravana.

In search of Sita, grief striken Rama with his brother moved towards a huge water-body named Pampasarovar. After many days of wandering they arrived at the bank of Pamapasarovar.

KISHKINDHA KANDA

This Kanda describes Rama's alliance with the community of locals known as Vanaras, meaning monkies, in his quest to find out his wife, Sita.

Crossing the Pampasarovara Rama with Lakshmana moved towards a mountain Rishyamuka. Here he met great monkey Hanumana and his master, exiled king of Kishkindha, Sugriva. Sugriva assured Rama of all his help in return of Rama's promise to kill his powerful brother Vali who had occupied the throne of Kishkindha and also took away his wife. Rama advises Sugriva to challenge Bali for fight. When Sugriva was wrestling with Vali and losing ground Rama from behind shot an arrow at Vali and killed him.

As promised Sugriva, now a king of Kishkindha, sent four teams of Vanaras in four directions to find out Sita. The team heading towards south was led by prince Angad, son of Vali, and Hanuman. Ultimately they arrived at Southern Ocean. Hanuman climbed over Mahendra mountain and made up his mind to jump over the great expanse of water and reach Lanka, kingdom of Ravana.

SUNDAR KANDA

He expanded his body and assumed a huge form and jumped up in the sky and started moving towards south with great speed.

To provide him a base to rest for a while the great Mainak mountain which was immersed in the ocean, rose above its surface. He requested the huge monkey to rest upon its golden peaks for a while. Hanuman told him that he was in hurry and to honour his request just touched one of its peak by hand and proceeded further.

Amazed by his feat the gods reqested powerful Nagamata Surasa to test the prowess of Hanumana. Assuming the form of sea—demoness Surasa stood in the mid-sea and threatened to swollow Haunuman. As Hanuman expanded his body far beyond the size of her open mouth Surasa too spread her mouth to match his size. The tussle went on. Sizing his opportunity Hanuman decreased his size equal to human thumb, jumped in her vastly open mouth and came out of it safely.

Pleased by his intelligence goddess Surasa appeared before him in her own true form and blessed him wishing him success in his efforts to find Sita.

Terrible demoness Simhika with immense size saw Hanuman moving through sky towards Lanka. She was endowed with the power to assume huge form at will and capture her prey just by holding to his shadow. She held the shadow of Hanuman floating on the waters of ocean and made him immobile.

When Hanuman saw down he saw a huge Chayagrahi demoness Simhika desirious of swollowing him alive. Angry Hanuman entered her mouth and hit at her heart region killing her instantly.

Moving through the sky he saw an island adorned with mountain ranges and green trees. Assuming his normal form he jumped down Lamba or Trikuta mountain. From there he saw the city of Lanka situated upon one of the high mountains on the shore of the ocean.

He decided to enter the city by night. As he stood before the main gate of Lanka, the city itself assuming the form of a great demoness stood in his way to resist his entry. Hamuman understood that she would not allow him to get into the city, he delivered a powerful slap to her and she fell down on the earth.

Hanuman jumped over the rampart and entered the city by night. He wandered through streets, mansions, houses of Lanka, even searched the palace of Ravana full of sleeping beauties. In the end he decided to enter Ashoka Vatika, pleasure garden of Ravana. After wandering in the garden he saw a thousand pillared, sparkling white Chaitya Prasad. Near it he saw Sita surrounded by several demonesses. At opportuned time Hanuman came down from the tree and stood before Sita. He assured her that Rama would soon rescue her from her captivity.

Elated by his success Hanuman destroyed the pleasure garden of Ravana and killed several demon warriors who came to capture him. Ultimately Ravana's son Indrajeet captured him and produced him before Ravana, king of Lanka. Hanuman asked him to release Sita or face consequences. Angry Ravana asked the demons to put his tail on fire and take him round the city for his subjects to see.

When the demons put fire to his tail Hanuman started jumping all over Lanka and put it to fire with the help of his burning tail. After doing that Hanuman, again jumping over the ocean, reached Mahendra mountain from where he started his expedition.

The team then returned to Kishkindha and reported the matter to Rama.

YUDDHA KANDA

Now the war. The enthusiastic army of monkies marched from Kishkindha and reached the shore of the southern ocean. Vibhishana, brother of Ravana, requested the demon king of Lanka to return Sita to Rama but furious Ravana rejected his advise. Vibhishana shunning Lanka joined Rama.

To cross the ocean the great monkey architect Nala built a bridge over it. Great war ensued in which Ravana, Kumbhakarana and Indrjeet lost their lives.

Vibhishana himself brought Sita in the presence of Rama. But Rama refused to accept her on the pretext that she lived in Ravana's abode which fact had defiled her. He asked her to go anywhere else and leave him.

Seeing this terrible sight gods rushed to Rama and depracating his behaviour as an ordinary human being, they reminded him that he was Bhagavan Narayan Deva himself. Here again there is a reference to Rama being the incarnation of Vishnu. Probably this reference to his divinity might have been later interpolation.

Bhagavan Agni himself brought Sita back from the fire in which she had jumped and vouching for her purity handed her over to Rama who accepted her with great joy. Rama returned to Ayodhya after which he was coronated as the king.

UTTAR KAND

This is the concluding part of the epic. It is generally believed that it was later interpolation. There is lot of background information about Ravana and other epic characters. It is related in this Khanda that Sita's character became suspect in the eyes of citizens of Ayodha hence Rama asked his brother Lakshmana to abandon pregnant Sita. He left her on the bank of Ganga from where Valmiki took her to his hermitage. She gave birth to two sons, Lava and Kusha, to whom Valmiki taught how to sing his epic. Rama decided to perform Ashvamedha in the Naimisharanya on the bank of river Gomati in which to entertain the guests the dancers and singers too were invited.

Valmiki too attened the Yajna in which Lava and Kusha sang his epic composition. Rama again insisted that Sita should undergo an ordial to prove her purity. Sita was brought to Yajna Mandapa. She uttered the vow that if she was pure let mother earth swollow her.

As soon as she uttered these words a beautiful and dazzling divine throne appeared from the earth which was carried over on their heads by great serpents. Along with the throne goddess of earth, Dharani Devi, too appeared. She lifted Sita with her arms and made her sit on jem-studded throne. Gradually they all went down in the Rasatala.

Rama in the end went towards the bank of river Sarayu and merged into Vaishna Tej or great circle of Vaishnava lustre, along with his brothers. Here Vishnu form of Rama was stressed indicating that Rama was an incarnation of Vishnu.

There are certain interesting legends in this Kanda such as Shatrughna founding the city of Madhupur which later became famous as Mathura. Pururava-Urvashi story, legend of king Yayati, Rama killing ascetic Shambuka belonging to Shudra caste, story of Vritrasura can be found in this chapter.

Rama katha became the part of number of Puranas and also the epic Mahabharata. Dramas too were written depicting full or part of Ramastory. Jain Ramayanas are category by themselves.

Several versions of Ramayana or the Story of Rama appeared in local regional languages in several parts of India. Kamba's Ramayana in Tamil was probably earliest which is ascribed to 9th century A.D. followed by Madhava Kandali's Assamese Ramayana which appeared in late 14th century. Most of the Ramayanas in different regional languages such as Gujarati, Brajabhasha, Avadhi, Malayalam, Marathi, Oriya, Rajasthani were written in 15th and 16th centuries, Ramacharitmanas of Tulasi being the most prominent of them all. Latest probably was Kashmiri Ramayana by Prakash Ram which appeared in 19th century.

However most amazing are the Ramayana versions that came up in different languages in South East Asian countries, each its own story to tell. This will give us some idea of how huge is the expance of Rama related mythology. Ramayanas got the status of religious scriptures since Rama came to be known as an incarnation of Vishnu.

N.P. Joshi in his Bharatiya Murtishastra writes that though there is no doubt about Ramayana being an ancient work, the cult of Rama as such took long time to formulate. We find no sculptural depiction of Rama story prior to Gupta period. Not only that we do not get even an independant image of Rama which could be ascribed to Gupta period. However, the tradition of sculpting the scenes from Rama story on temple walls was quite old.

During the period beginning from 7th century A.D. and ending with 14th century A.D., N.P. Joshi points out that, in the North India Rama is seen in Dashavatara panels. We find two independant sculptures of Rama at Khajuraho. Though we see the depiction of Rama story in sculptural form on temples, we do not come across independant Rama temples as such. However in works on iconography we get number of descriptions of how to sculpt Rama images in different forms, we seldom find images answering to literary descriptions.

The bronze images of Chola period of Rama, Sita, Lakshmana, etc. are class by themselves. 17th century Saint Ramadas of Maharashtra is credited with building the temples of Hanuman and Rama all over the region. Rama temple at Chaphal is very famous, equally famous are the Rama temples at Nasik on the bank of river Godavari which in ancient times was known as Panchavati.

Ayodhya in North India is having several Rama temples. The temple at Rama Janma Bhumi or birth place of Rama was converted into Masjid during the reign of Moughal emperor Babur. That means there must have been temple dedicated to Rama at Janma Bhumi at least in early 16th century or even earlier.

Hajari Rama temple at Vijayanagara in Karnataka was possibly built by 15th century king Virupaksha II. (According to some king Krishna "Deva Raya) It is modest but perfect specimen of Vijayanagara style of temple building. It's walls are covered with relief scenes from the Ramayana.

In Jammu there is a magnificent temple of Rama known as Raghunatha Mandir. Mithila-Janakpur is considered as birth-place of Sita. Here there are temples dedicated to Sita, Rama, Lakshmana. There are many places here which are mythically associated with the life of Sita. In the city of Sitamadhi there is a temple of Sita and also of Rama, Lakshmana.

Chitrakuta in central India has many sacred places connected with Rama Katha. Around Rameshvara in South we find some temples dedicated to Rama, Sita, etc. and also many sacred places associated with Rama Katha. It is believed that Shiva Linga at Rameshvaram temple was established by Rama himself. From island of Rameshvara to Lanka there is a sandstone mountain range below the surface of sea. It is considered to be the relic of the bridge Rama built across the sea to reach Lanka.

Ramtek is a historical place and a temple city in the Vidarbha region of Maharashtra known for 1500 years. It is believed that Rama rested on a hill here for sometime during his exile. Hence it came to be known as Ramgiri. Local legend is that in ancient times on this hill Rama's paduka (footwear) used to be worshipped, however it was replaced later with the images of Rama, Sita and Lakshmana and temple was built to house them. Dynasty of Vakataka was devoted to Rama and they made grants to this temple.

There is a hill on the border of Madhya Pradesh and Bihar known as Ramgarh. Describing its location T. Bloch writes. 'It is situated in the Lakhapur Zamindari of the Sirguja state, 100 miles distant from the nearest railway station, Kharsia, on the Bengal-Nagour line.' There are a few caves on the hill, one among them is known as Sitabenga. In it an inscription ascribed to 3rd century B.C. was found. According to local legend the name of the hill, Ramgarh, indicates that Rama must have lived here during his exile for some time. The name of the cave Sitabenga on it underlines Sita's association with it. Some scholars believe this is the same hill described by Kalidasa in Meghaduta as Ramagiri where Sita used to take bath during her sojourn.

Hampi in Karnataka in ancient times was known as Kishkindha and river Tungabhadra as Pampasaroar. In the book The Vijayanagar Empire edited by Vasundhara Filliozat it is stated that 'even today when we go to Chitamanimatha in Anegondi people show us a place where Rama had killed Vali hiding behind the trees and enthroned Sugriva. According to Pampamahatmya, on the southern bank of Tungabhadra is a tank locally known as Sitakonda. Sita bathed here when Ravana was carrying her to Lanka. This tank is near Kodandarama temple at Hampi. Here Rama met Hanuman and set him to meet Sita in Lanka. Apart from these, on natural stone pavements some long lines are seen and they are known as 'Sitaseragu' or Sita's sari. (p. 2).

Some prominent scholars, including H.D. Sankalia, are of the opinion that Ravana's Lanka was somewhere in the Vindya mountains infested with number of tribal communities, some of whom still adore Ravana and consider him as their ancestor.

It is believed that Rama was born on ninth lunar day in the bright fortnight of the month of Chaitra. This day is popularly known as Ramnavami and celebrated all over the country with great enthusiasm. Ayodhya is the main centre of this festival. Dr. B.N. Sharma in his Festivals of India writes. 'At Shri Varadaraja Perumal temple in Pondicherry town, the festival of Ramnavami is celebrated by thousands of devotees for twenty days in the Tamil month of Panguni (March-April). A highly decorated procession of Sri Rama, Sita, Lakshmana, Hanumana is taken out in the important streets of the city.' (p. 74).

On Ashvin shuddha dashami a festival, popularly known as Dussehra is grandly celebrated all over the country. It is believed that on this day Rama achieved victory over Ravana. The huge effigies of demons Ravana, Kumbhakarna and Meghnada are burnt in a public ceremony and Ramlila plays are enacted in North India.

There is a huge literature related to Rama. This incarnation of Vishnu is specially remembered for sterling human qualities and ideals upheld by him. A Upanishada named Ramapurvatapaniya, attached to Atharva Veda, was composed to extol Rama. In it the Mantra and Yantra of Rama is included. Here again Rama is considered as an incarnation of Vishnu.

Rama Katha did not remain confined to literature only but manifested through different media such as sculpture, painting and through different performing art forms as well as dramatic enactments. Earliest glimpses of it could be seen in Valmiki Ramayana itself.

After composing Ramayana in the verse form Valmiki set it to music and taught two of his disciples, Lava and Kusha, how to sing it dramatically, on the accompaniment of a stringed musical instrument called Tantri, in the Margi style.

Marga as opposed to Deshya (folk) is a term used for classical mode of performance. Another meaning of Marga is way, path, passage, road. Hence, Margi could be street theatre and as such Lava and Kusha sang it in lanes, bylanes, roads of Ayodhya.

Some scholars take the words Kusha and Lava in the sence of Kushilavas meaning bard, herald, actor. They feel that Kushilavas took up the performance of the epic in later period. This street theatre tradition was converted into dramatic performance in due course.

It was in Harivamsha Purana there is an elaborate description of dramatisation of Ramayana epic (Ramayanam mahakavyamuddishya natakam kritam) in which Rama was described as an incarnation of Vishnu. This Purana is ascribed to third century A.D.

Around the same time Bhasa wrote two Rama plays, Pratima and Abhisheka Natakas, in which Rama is recognised as an incarnation Bhagavan Narayana. Kerala developed a style of staging Sanskrit plays which is known as Kutiyattam. These two plays are still enacted on Kutiyattam stage. These two plays along with Shaktibhadras Asharyachudami cover the entire story of Ramayana. It is said that once Rama story based Mahanataka too was part of Kutiyattam repertory.

After Bhasa the prominent playwright of 7th century A.D), Bhavabhuti wrote two Rama plays - Mahaviracharita and Uttara Rama Charita. After him came the spate of Rama plays, some of whom were clearly influenced by him. Bhavabhuti's patron king, Yashovarman, wrote a play Ramabhyudaya. Immediately after that two Kalacheri kings, Bhimata and Mayuraj, wrote Rama plays titled Swapnadashanana and Udattaraghava respectively.

Murari, last quarter of eighth century, wrote a play Anargharaghavaon Ramayana theme declaring himself to be Bala Valmiki or Junior Valmiki. Poet Rajashekhara who hailed from the place called Vatsagulma wrote in the 10th century an extensive Rama play with ten acts declaring himself as an incarnation of Valmiki and Bhavabhuti. In his Balaramayana he had made infatuation of Ravana for Sita the dominating theme. In one act he had made use of string puppets.

We have a peculiar literary text, described as Nataka or drama, found in two versions respectively titled as Hanumannataka and Mahanataka. In the Bhoja Prabandha of Ballal Sen a legend is found about this work. It says that Hanumana himself wrote this work and then inscribed it on the stone with his nails. When Valmiki saw it it gave him jitters. He thought that if Hanumana's work gets circulated his own Ramayana, will pale into insignificance. Hence, he persuaded Hanumana to throw it in the sea. Hanumana did exactly that.

During the reign of King Bhoja of Dhara Nagari some sea-divers discovered some portion of the work inscribed on stone pieces. When they were presented before king he ordered his court poet Damodar Mishra to resurrect it.

Bhoja and his court poet are ascribed to 11th century. But it seems that some additions were made in it in later times also.

It is said that this text was dramatically staged in Kutiyattam style in Kerala.

Rama plays continued to be written. Above mentioned works are prominent—Rama plays in sanskrit.

In Kerala an exclusive form of Rama theatre emerged in 17th century inspired by Vira Kerala Varma, the chieftan of the principality of Kottarakara, who was also known as Kottarakara Thampuran. Named as Ramanattam it consisted of cycle of eight plays depicting Rama story. Gradually it evolved into Kathakali theatre incorporating stories from many epical and Puranic source. However there were number of Rama story based plays in the repertory of

Kathakali. As recently as 1969 a play Sampurna Ramayana was written by C.A.A.Warier and staged by P.S.V. Natyasangham Kathakali Company. In this play the Rama story from his birth to coronation as a king of Ayodhya is related. (The Kathakali Complex, p. 12-23)

An interesting legend regarding the enactment of Kathakali play based on Rama story at Rama temple of Tiru-vilva-mala recorded by K. Bharatha Iyer in his book, Kathakali. Iyer writes :

'Acting in the true sense of the word as understood in India, is not mere impersonation, however clever or illusionistic the effect. The actor is compared to the Yogi, meaning thereby that he treads the path of Yoga (Union) or mental concentration, whereby the subject and the object, worshipper and the worshipped, the actor and the acted become one. Kerala legends emphasise this aspect. In the temple at Tiru-vilva-mala (In Tr.-Cochin state), where the presiding deity is Rama, episodes from the favourite Rama plays enacted. Once when Khara Vadha (slaying of demon Khara by Rama) was being enacted, Khara burst on the scene with highly provocative challenge to Rama. He mocked, sneered, proudly boasted of his great prowess. In mountaining rage he raised war cries that sounded like monsoon thunder creating a tense electric atmosphere of blood and fury. The dreaded and vicious demon appeared ready to destroy everything before him. The audience cowered, weighed down by the sense of an impending doom and Asura towered over all, fury incarnate. 'You worm come to fight with me', sneered the demon. He was no longer an actor simulating a role; he had become Khara himself. Suddenly the doors of the inner shrine flew open and a column of bright flame blinded everyone for a spece of a split second. When the audience recovered from their state of shock, Khara was missing. The enactment of this particular play was discontinued in the temple from that day (p. 26).

In Indian folk and classical dance styles as well as traditional theatre forms such as Yakshagana, Ankia Nat, Jatra enactment of Rama story is quite popular. However it is Ramlila theatre of North India which is exclusively devoted to depiction of Rama story.

It is believed that Saint Tulsidas made the beginning of Ramlila tradition organising a tableau, Janki, of Rama's cornation at Assi ka Ghat on river Ganga at Varanasi on the Sharad Purnima day sometimes in 17th century A.D.

Ramlila is enacted in different formats all over North India every year a few days before Dassehra, the day on which grand finale in the form of burning the effigies of Ravana, Kumbhakarana and Meghanada. Most famous of all Ramlilas is one enacted on huge ground of Ramnagar near Varanasi.

In the ground various locales described in the Ramayana are marked and day after day the action move from one locale to another for about forty days. It is a unique dramatic experience.

Delhi is yet another place where most glamorous exhibition of Ramlilas take place at number of localities.

India is described as a Home of Puppet Theatre by the scholars. It was here, indeed, the art of puppetry originated. However a legend that prevailed in Karnataka ascribes it's origin to Rama, prince of Ayodhya.

The legend says that Rama gave this art to boatman Guha who ferried him across Ganga. Guha in turn passed it on to the Killekyatas, the community of itinerant puppeteers of Karnataka, who had migrated from their original habitation in the Maharashtra.

K.S. Upadyaya writes; 'Leather puppetry is associated especially with the Killekyata community. There is a belief that Guha, the man who ferried Sri Ram across Ganga when he set out for forest, is the one who gave it (art of puppetry) to Killekyatas. Guha had it from Sri Rama himself as a reward for his loyalty. Significantly, each family generally names its first son as Rama or Ramayya. The art itself is known as Gombe-ramar-ata.' (Sangeet Natak, No. 98, p. 10)

Even today the Karnataka puppeteers have number of puppet plays based on Rāmayana themes.

In the Sanskrit dramatic literature there are certain plays which are described as Chhaya Natakas or call themselves as such. There is lot of controversy about the term Chhaya Nataka but there are some scholars who translates it as shadow plays.

In this genre are the plays like Mahanataka by Hanuman (9th century A.D.), Dutangada of Subhata and Ullagharaghava of Someshvara (both ascribed to 13th century), etc. are shadow plays based on Rama-Katha.

In India all the four forms of traditional puppetry - string, shadow, glove and rod) - are found. Except for the string puppetry of Rajasthan other forms have Ramayana plays in their repertory. But there are two forms of shadow puppetry - Ravana Chhaya of Karnataka and Thol Pava Koothu of Kerala - which are exclusively devoted to narrating the Rama story on the screen.

The nomenclature of Rama story based shadow theatre of Orissa as a Ravana Chhaya is rather curious. However there are explanations for that. Rama being luminious divinity do not cast his shadow on any surface. The puppet representing Ravana is much larger than that of Rama and also more boldly and dramatically conceived, says Jivan Pani.

Jivan Pani who wrote a monograph on Ravana Chhaya has yet another explaination for the said nomenclature. He feels that this form of shadow theatre might have come under Jain and Buddhist influence in its formative period. Jain Rama stories do not paint Ravana as demon king but Prati-Vasudeva. In some "Buddhist works like Lankavatarasutra (Dharmakirti, 6th century A.D.) paints Ravana as an ideal Buddhist king (p. 16).

However this influence remained confined to the name of the shadow theatre form. As Pani has pointed out Orissa has a strong Ramayana tradition, specially in the field of literature. While there are only 3 to 4 versions of Mahabharata more than 50 versions of Ramayana are found in Oriya written under the influence of Valmiki Ramayana. Some of them are very lyrical and can be sung and acted. One among them is Vichitra Ramayana by medieval Oriya poet Vishvanatha Khuntia. It is this Ramayana which forms the texual base of Ravana Chhaya and in it Ravana is not glorified.

In the Kerala there is a traditional shadow theatre form which is known as Tol-pava-koothu which is exclusively devoted to shadow playing Rama story. In the premises of Bhagavati temples small brick-built structures known as Koothumadam are raised facing the temple. A screen is put across and shadow plays are enacted unfolding Rama story for number of days. It is a ritual enacted to appease goddess Bhadrakali.

It is believed when Rama-Ravana war was in progress goddess Bhadrakali was busy elsewhere killing the terrible demon Darika. This deprived her of the opportunity to enjoy the thrills of Rama-Ravana combat. This is made up by screening for her the shadow plays woven around Rama story ending in the great battle. Kamban's Ramayana forms the textual base of these plays which, in older days, were enacted for fortyone days as a part of Bhagavati temple festival.

In India since ancient times there flourished a strong tradition of picture-showmen who would narrate a story with the help of paintings. In olden times they were known as Mankhas. This tradition has still survived in some parts of the country. Patuas of West Bengal, Garodas of Gujrat, Chitrakathis of Maharashtra—all picture showmen—narrate Rama story with the help of paintings. Similar tradition survives in the Andhra Pradesh also.

9

BALARAMA

Some Puranic works have listed Balarama or Sankarshana, elder brother of Krishna, as an incarnation of Vishnu. Jayadeva subscribed to this view by counting him among the incarnations of Vishnu. In his Gita Govinda's Dashavatar Ashtapadi he says :

> On your beautiful body you are wearing cloths resembling clouds full of rain
>
> They look like Yamuna who came near you frightened by the power of your plough
>
> O Keshava in Haladhara form Victory to you Jagadisha Hare

Narrating in his Abhinaya Darpana the symbolic gesture to indicate Balarama, Acharya Nandikeshvara says :

> Right hand in Patak and left in Musti Hasta Mudra.

In popular perception Balarama was an incarnation of serpent Shesha on whose coils Vishnu rests. Describing his final departure the Vishnu Purana says that when his end came he sat under a tree in the Prabhasa Kshetra. From his mouth a very big serpent came out. Siddhas and Nagas offered worship to him, then he moved towards the ocean. Ocean himself appeared before him by taking arghya, water for worship, in his hands. Worshipped by prominent serpents he entered the ocean.

In the Dashama Skhandha of Bhagavata Purana it is said that as a seventh child the great serpent Ananta also known as Shesha entered the womb of Devaki, mother of

Krishna and wife of Vasudeva languishing in the prison of Kamsa, the cruel demonic ruler of Mathura. Krishna asked his Yogamaya, the yogic power, to extract the child from the womb of Devaki and put him in the womb of Vasudeva's second wife living in cowherd settlement of Gokula. As he was extracted from the womb of Devaki he came to be known as Sankarshana. Bhagavata says that due to his quality of Lokaranjana, charming the people he became famous as Ram and he was top among men of strength he came to be known as Balabhadra.

Ananta or Shesha is considered as 'ansha' of Vishnu himself hence he might have been ennumerated among incarnations of Vishnu,

Serpent worship was prevalent in India since ancient times. Mathura region was one of the prominent centres of cult of serpents. Dr. Vasudevasharan Agrawala opines that we find large number of Yaksha and Naga sculptures belonging to Mathura art of Shunga and Kushana period. Folk festivals dedicated to these deities were known Yakshamaha and Nagamaha respectively. He refers to colossal Naga image from Chadgaon. Naga is in human form with serpent hood spread over his head. (Bharatiya Kala, p. 258).

An inscription worded in mixed Prakrit and Sanskrit found at Mathura and ascribed to first or second century A.D. throws light on cult of Nagas in the region and also about activities of the actor brothers who used to perform the roles of Sankarshana and Krishna-Vasudeva. The inscription states :

> Success: In the year (illegible), on the fifth, on the aforementioned date the shrine of the blessed Dhadikarna, Lord of the Serpents, a stone slab was set up by the boys headed by Nandabala, the sons of those actors (sailalakas) of Mathura who are being praised as Chadaka brothers. By the merit of this gift be for their parents, preferably: may it be for the welfare and

happiness of all beings. (Epiraphia Indica I (1892), p. 37-93)

Dhadikarna's name occurs in the Harivamsha in the list of righteous and beneficent nagas, invoked in a prayer which Sankarshana himself said to have composed. Harivansha is an appendix of the epic Mahabharata. Dr. Agrawala states in his book Bharatiya Kala (p. 258) that in the images of Nagadevatas found in Mathura region one small image was of Dhadhikarna Nag. In the inscription Dhadhikarna is addressed as Nagendra and in Harivamsha he is referred to as Nagaraja, king of serpents. The importance of Naga cult can be gauged by the fact that there were shrines dedicated to serpent deities of various descriptions as also they had a good following.

Dr. Norvin Hein in his book the Miracle plays of Mathura (p. 233-36) has put up a theory that actors, Chandaka brothers, were called so because they used to enact the roles of Sankarshana and Vasudeva-Krisha who belonged to luner family he says: 'What does Chandaka mean. It is prakritization of the Sanskrit Chandraka, the adjective derived from the noun Chandra, the moon. So Chandraka means luner, and our actors are being called 'The Luner Brothers'. Why ? Because they are famous for their performance of the roles of the pair who are luner brothers par excellence: Sankarshana and Krishna.

Explaining his position further he refers to Naneghat inscription of first century B.C. by a Satavahana queen on the wall of the cave in Western India. Here we find invocation to her favourite gods at the beginning.

The inscription says: '(Om adoration) to Dharma (the Lord of created beings): adoration to Indra, adoration to Sankarshana and Vasudeva, the decendants of moon (chandasutanam) who are endowed with majesty... (Archaeological Survery of Western India, 5(1883), 60 f.

Hein says: 'The phrase 'Sankarshana and Vasudeva, candasutanam enables us to say with confidence that the Chadaka brothers of Mathura inscription were actors in Mathura mystry plays, famous for their portarayal of the two leading personalities of the older Krishnaite mythology, Sankarshana and his brother Vasudeva and Krishna.

It is interesting to note that the actor community of Mathura who enacted Krishnalila plays belonged to the Cult of Serpents. In the Vishnuparva of Harivamsha Purana there is a detailed description of pleasue trip of Yadavas to seashore. Adance troupe enacted various lilas of Krishna and Balrama to amuse the Yadavas: Actors assumed the role of Revati and Balarama: Spelendorous Balarama (actor in his guise), quite intoxicated from drinking liquor, leaped about with his wife, the daughter of king Revata, to the sweet and even rhythm of clapping hands.

Balarama was famous for his excessive fondness for strong liquors. Vishnu Purana says: Once Balarama desired to meet his erstwhile cowherd family and friends of Vrindavan. He was received with joy by the cowherd community on his arrival. One day they all, gopa and gopies, went to Vrindav forest. By the order of Bhagavan Varuna the Varuni started flowing from locally grown Kadamba tree and Balarama drank it to his heart's content along with cowherd boys and girls, expert in dance and music.

In his stupor Balarama ordered river Yamuna to come close as he wanted to take bath in her cool waters. But Yamuna ignored him. Angry Balarama dragged her course to him by the tip of his plough. Frightened Yamuna appeared before him in person asking for his pardon. Changing her course she started flowing from near the place where Balarama was camping with his friends.

In the Braj region there is a village Ramghat, on the bank of river Yamuna. There is a temple of Balarama in the village. It is locally believed that it was here Balarama drank liquor, performed Ras with cowherd boys and girls and made

Yamuna charge her course. You can still see here the changed course of Yamuna.

There are number of temples dedicated to Balarama in Braj region but one at Baldeva gaon is very famous. Ancient image of Balarama was found in a tank here. It is considered as one of the oldest images ever found in Braj region. A temple was built to house the image. In the corner of the sanctum there is a lifesize image of Revati, his wife.

Vijaya, that is intoxicant Bhang, is offered to Balarama as a part of daily worship. Most boisterous form of Holi is played here in which women pull the cloths from the back of men and then beat them up by making whip of the same, colours flying in all directions. Holi of villages Jab-Bathain is held on the bank of Balabhadra kunda where women beat men with long sticks and men protect themselves by taking the cover of thorny branches of Babhul trees.

Earliest known reference to the Cult of Balarama-Sankarshana is found in Arthashastra of Kautilya ascribed to fourth century B.C. Arthashastra says:

> Spies disguised as ascetics with shaved heads or braided hair pretending to be the worshippers of god Sankarshana may mix their sacrificial beverage with the juice of Madana plant (and give to the cowherds) and carry off the cattle.

P. Banerjee in his The Life of Krishna in Indian Art commenting on this passage says: 'While we recognise two of the Vyuhas, namely Sankarshana and Vasudeva in the Gosundi and Naneghat inscriptions, it is interesting to note that both the inscriptions mention Sankarshana first and Vasudeva second though, according to the Vyuha doctrine Vasudeva is highest self and Sankarshana is an emanation from him. Historically, Sankarshana is the elder brother of Krishna and initially he had independant cult and equal position as that of Vasudeva. (p. 9).

However the reference to the cult of Balarama in the Arthashastra is so scanty that we can not glean much information from it. However the information that Balarama had seperate cult is very important.

R.G.Bhandarkar in his book Vaisnavism, Saivism and Minor religious Systems (p: 3) refers to Buddhist work Niddesa which gives the list of various religious systems and superstitions that prevailed in the fourth century B.C. Here worshippers of Vasudeva and Baladeva are mentioned. Probably each had seperate following. The Mahabharata speak Vasudeva-Vargya to signify followers of Vasudeva.

Bhasa is first known playwright of India who is credited with writing some 13 plays. He is ascribed to 4th-5th century B.C. by some scholars. Swapnavasavadatta is one of his more famous plays. The opening prayer song of this play is dedicated to Balarama. It says:

> 'The arms of Balarama having the lustre of just risen moon, looking like lotus flower, sometimes hanging lazily due to excessive drinking protect you all. May Balarama who looks as beautiful as Vasanta ritu itself, bless you:'

In his plays Urubhangam and Balacharitara we find the character of Balarama appearing on the stage, though briefly.

It seems that Cult of Balararaa was in vogue since 4th-5th centuries B.C. and according to Arthashastra and Niddesa had independant following. Probably this ancient Naga deity was later incorporated in Vaishnava fold by adopting him as a elder brother of Krishna-Vasudeva.

As far as known literary and inscriptional evidence shows there does not seem to have any reference to liquor drinking of Nagas. Probably Balarama might have imbibed this trait from the cult of Yakshas. Yakshas were fond of drinking wine as depicted by Kalidasa in his Meghaduta. In Mathura region number of images of Kubera Vaishravana, king of Yakshas, were found. He was shown drinking liquor.

This cult was very popular in Mathura region. Balarama, it seems, combined in himself the traits of Naga and Yaksha cults.

F.S. Growse in his Mathura : A District Memoir says that: 'Balaram, under the name Belus, is described by Latin writers as the Indian Hercules, and said to be one of the tutelary divinities of Mathura (p. 59).

Inscriptional and literary references show that around the beginning of Christian era Bhagavata religion whose main pillars were Vasudeva-Krishna and Sankarshana-Balarama grew fast. If they had two seperate cults in historic past they merged into one, on the day when Balarama was accepted in Bhagavata fold as elder brother of Krishna. Due to him carrying pestal and plough some take him on deity of agriculture.

Balarama played role supportive to Krishna, his younger brother, practically merging his personality into his. However we see some quick flashes of his independant nature which led to difference of opinion between the two also.

Puranas, including Bhagavata, sketches his eventful childhood he spent in cowherd settlements of Gokul and Vrindavan. He did kill some demons like Dhenuka, monkey terror Dvivida, Pralambasura, fought by the side of his broter with Jarasandha, Emperor of Magadha, and his huge army, which attacked Mathura for eighteen times and repelled their invasion. He married beautiful Revati, daughter of king Revata and remained faithful to her.

There are number of stories about inhuman strength of Balarama. Samba, son of Jambavati and Krishna was quite adventurous and reckless, Duryodhana, prince of Hastinapura, had a beautiful daughter by name Lakshmana. When Samba came to know about her Swayamvara he went to Hastinapur and forcefully took her away. Angry

Duryodhana along with Kaurava warriors persuded him and brought him back to Hastinapur as a captive.

Balarama went to Hastinapura to pacify the Kauravas but they refused to hand over Samba and his bride to him.

Angry Balarama simply uprooted the city of Hastinapur by his weapon, the plough, and started dragging it towards Ganga to drown it in the river. Kuruvamshis, frightened by the act of mighty Balarama surrendered to him and asked for his pardon. They offered him prayers and said that he was none else but Shesha having thousands and thousands heads on which rests the earth. However when Arjuna took off with his sister subhadra he got furious only to be pacified by Krishna.

Rukmi was son of Bhishmaka, king of Vidarbha with capital at Kundinpur. Krishna kidnapped his sister on her own request and moved away in his chariot. Rukmi persued them with huge army but Krishna defeated him. Insulted by this defeat he vowed not to return to Kundinpur. He founded a city named Bhojakataka and started living there.

Once king of Kalinga advised Rukmi to challange Balarama for a game of dice. They knew that Balarama was not a good dice player. Balarama reluctantly accepted the challenge as was considered honourable those days. Rukmi won the first round. Encouraged by that he started playing second round with big stakes. As luck would have it Balarama won that round.

But Rukmi and King of Kalinga refused to accept the defeat. All the king in the gambling hall supported Rukmi. A divine voice proclaimed the victory of Balarama but Rukmi wont relent.

Balarama became furious and with one blow of his pestle killed Rukmi.

Suta is a narrator of ancient ballads and epic poems known as Itihasa, Purana, Akhyana, etc. Taittiriya Brahmana describes him as a singer. Balarama was not in favour of participating in Bharata war taking sides so he went for pilgrimage. In the course of his wandering he came to Naimisharanya where Rishis were performing a Satra.

Balarama saw Suta Lomaharshana, disciple of Maharshi Vyasa was sitting on raised platform to narrate Itihasa, Purana to the Rishis who were sitting on floor. This infuriated Balarama.

He said Though of low cast you are sitting up above us who are custodians of Dharma so you must be given death punishment. Being the disciple of Vyasa you have studied Itihasa, Purana, Dharmashastra and other sacred works. But you have no control over yourself and humility in nature. You are considering yourself to be great scholar showing false pride. Like all the action of actor is nothing but counterfeiting, your discouses are nothing but sham. They profit nobody. Those who wear symbols of religion but do not observe it in action are worth killing.

Saying this Balarama hit him with pointed sacred Kusha grass. Poor Suta died instantly. Rishi Munis did not approve of the killing. They opined that he has committed a sin equal to Brahma-hatya or killing a Brahmin. He was asked to undergo a penance to atone for the sin.

Repenting for his rash action Balarama said that in the place of Lomaharshana his son will continue narrating the Puranas and for that he would give him long life and strength to perform his vocation.

As a atonement of his action Balarama agreed to kill a demon Bilvala, son of Ilvala who was troubling the Rishis of Naimisharanya. One day Bilvala appeared in the sky and started throwing dust and other impurities upon Yajna performing Rishis. Balarama dragged him on earth with his plough and killed him with the blow of pestle.

Balarama was blunt, outspoken and brutally frank in voicing his opinion. In the beginning of Udyoga Parva we are told that the supporters of Pandavas assebled in the court of King Virata of Matsya Country to chalk out a plan to get their share of kingdom from Kauravas. The meeting opened with the speech of Krishna who in the end suggested that Pandavas should send someone as emissary to Kauravas with the message to return their share who they had seized by wrong means.

Balarama agreed to this proposal but said that the messanger should put their proposal humbly before the Kauravas. Because Pandavas too were more at fault and responsible for losing their kingdom.

Balarama said that Yudhisthir did not know the game of dice. Even after the opposition of his brothers he played the game of dice with Shakuni, son of king of Gandhara. Though there were several gamblers in the Kaurava court Yudhishtir challanged Shakuni, known expert in gambling, and went on playing with him. When he started losing the game he obstinately continued playing and invited defeat. It was no fault of Shakuni that Yudhisthira lost the game and his kingdom too.

This was too much for the warriors on Pandava's side. But what Balarama said was true.

Peace efforts failed. Terrible war broke out between cousins which is known to history as Bharata War. Krishna did not actually took up arms on the side of Pandavas but played great role in planning the clever moves. Yadava army fought on the side of Kauravas. Balarama left Dwaraka and went on pilgrimage.

When Balarama returned after knowing about Bharata war it was the last chapter of the bloody conflict and his two disciples - Bhimasena and Duryodhana - were about to fight a duel with their respective maces. Balarama suggested Samantapanchak Tirtha near Kurukshetra as a venue.

The mace fight started and Bhima started losing the ground. On the suggestion of Krishna his friend Arjuna signalled Bhima to hit Duryodhana on his left thigh and when he did it like that Duryodhana, though better warrior, fell on the ground defeated.

This infuriated mighty Balarama because according to the rules of mace fight hitting the adversary by mace below the navel was not permissible. Bhima's hitting fallen Duryodhana on head by his feet made him still angry. He rushed towards Bhimasena lifting up his weapon, the plough, but Krishna stopped him.

Krishna spoke with Balarama in support of Bhima but he was not satisfied by clever and crafty talk of his younger brother and critisised Bhima for his Cowerdly act and left for Dwaraka.

In the concluding portion of the Mahabharata there is a chapter titled Mausal Parva.lt narrates the tragic story of annihilation of Andhakas and Vrishnis of Dwaraka. Upset by terrible curse of Brahmanas and seeing ill omens plauging Dwaraka Krishna asked his kinsmen to leave the city for some time and go to Prabhasa Tirtha on seashore on pilgrimage.

Yadavas turned the event into great picnic. With delicious food and variety of drinks they camped on the seashore with actors, dancers, musicians in attendance for entertainment. Watching the performances of Nata, Nartaka the 'mahapana', great drinking marathon of Yadavas started. Right in front of Krishna the Vrishni warriors started drinking, Balarama being one among them. Suddenly under the influence of liquor they started quarelling among themselves and killed each other without mercy. Balarama and Krishna escaped the fate but ended their life seperately.

Balarama achieved the status of an incarnation. He was expert in mace fight, Gada Yuddha, Bhima and Duryodhana were his disciples. He was greatly fond of drinking. Fair of complexion he used to wear only one single ear ring in either of his ears and had a liking for blue cloths.

N.P. Joshi in his Bharatiya Murtishastra states that the worship of Balarama was prevalent in Mathura, Varanasi and Gwalior regions since Shunga period. Stone images of Balarama, holding the weapons plough and musala, and Nagas spreading their hoods over his head, belonging to this period were found in the area of the influence of his cult.

Since Kushana period we start getting Balarama images holding the cups of liquor. One such image was found at Sadabad, Mathura, now housed in the Mathura Museum. It is a powerful sculpture with serpent hood spread over the head of the deity and a cup of liquor in his left hand. He is adorned with a few ornaments and a Vanamala, garland of forest flowers, is seen running around the neck to his feet.

He is seen along with Krishna in some Krishna-lila sculptures. In one such sculpture they are seen engaged in wrestling bout with the wrestlers of Kamsa.

Early depiction of Balarama, carrying his mace and plough, along with Krishna on other side is found on the bronze coin of king Agathocles ascribed to second century B.C. This king ruled from Taxila over large part of Indian territory.

It is evident from an inscription ascribed to first century B.C., found at Ghosundi in Chittorgarh district, that shrines were erected in the honour of Sankarshana and Vasudeva. Mora (near Mathura) stone inscription of the same period refers to images of Bhagavata Vrishni Panchaviras of which Balarama was part, beautifully carved in stone. Tradition of sculphing panels showing Balarama, Krishna, and Ekanansha goes back to Kushana period.

Very few images of Balarama belonging to Gupta period were found. It indicates the decline of Balarama cult. N.P. Joshi writes that on a terracotta plaque found at Chandausi in Uttar Pradesh Balarama is shown fighting with Pralambhasura. In one scene sculpted on Lakshmana temple at Sirpur, Madhya Pradesh, Balarama is shown killing Suta

Lomaharshana. At Mandhal in Nagpur district an image of Balarama killing Dhenuka is found.

Writing about medieval art of eastern part of India N.P. Joshi writes that independant images of Balarama, even in bronze, are found in this period. The image of Balarama with Ekanansha and Krishna was made during the rule of Pal king Mahipal. In the art of Central and Western region independant images of Balarama were sculpted. In the central Indian art he is shown as an incarnation of Vishnu. He is seen with serpent hood, pestle, plough, cup of liquor.

In the National Museum, New Delhi, a Balarama image, having his name inscribed on it is housed. Made in black stone he is shown holding, conch, lotus, mace and disk. The images of Balarama and Revati are shown sculpted on a temple at Kardameshvar, near Varanasi, ascribed to Pratihara period. In the Lucknow Museum there is a beautiful image of Balarama along with Ekanansha and Krishna. In Rajasthan he is seen placing his hand around the neck of Madiravahika (female bearer of liquor) or with Revati. At Khajuraho too we see his sculptures.

The most sacred and famous wooden image of Balarama along with Subhadra and Krishna is found on the Ratnasimhasana of Jagannatha temple at Puri.

10

KRISHNA

Dynamic dark-hued Krishna is the nucleus of Bhagavata religion constantly generating myths, legends, stories in space and time, His standing in Avatara pantheon is supreme. He is not just any ansha-vatara, part-incarnation, but purna-vatara, total incarnation. Bhagavata Purana moves a step forward and says - Krishnastu Bhagavan Swayam. Poet Jayadeva in his Gita (Govinda states that all the incarnations originated in Krishna himself. He says:

Keshawa: ghritadashavidha rupa Jaya Jagadisha Hare

Dashakrutikrute Krishnaya tubhyam namah!

Describing the mudra indicating Krishna Acharya Nandikeshvara in his Abhinayadarpana says:

Both the hands in Mrigashirsha facing each other; held in front of the mouth.

Mahabharata is the first and earliest known biography of Krishna. It opens with the words Natayanam namaskritya meaning I bow before you O Narayana Vishnu-Krisha. The narrator of the epic Ugrashrava Sauti further informs his august audience assembled in deep woods of Naimisha, that composed by Maharshi Vedavyasa it narrates the ancient story of Bhagavan Vasudeva-Krishna - Bhagavan Vasudevasya kirtyatetra sanatana. 'What I am narrating here is the eternal saga of Lord Vasudeva-Krishna which is sacred and delightful to listen, 'says Sauti in the very first Parva of the epic. Krishna is the nucleus around which the epic was woven. No wonder the well known twelfth century Belava inscription in addition to calling him Gopi-Shata-

Kelikara rightfully calls him Mahabharata Sutradhar or string-holder of Mahabharata.

When Vedavyasa calls the story of Vasudeva Krishna as Sanatana or ancient one it must have been certainly older than his epic composition. We find the name Krishna mentioned in the Vedic literature but we are not certain it refers to Vasudeva Krishna of the Mahabharata.

Some scholars believe that Krishna, black and bountiful like rain cloud, was popular deity of aborginals. May be due to that Aryan Rig Veda refers to him as Asura. It says :

'The swift moving Krishna with ten thousand (demons) stood on the Amshumati; by his might Indra caught him shorting (in water); benevolent to man, smote his malicious (band).

'I have seen the swift moving (demon) lurking in an inaccessible place in the depth of river Amshumati. I have seen Krishna standing there as (the sun) in the cloud. I appeal to you showerer; conquer him in battle.

'Then the swift moving one shining forth assumed his own body by the Amshumati and Indra and Brihaspati and his ally smote the Godless hosts as they drew near. (RV VIII 996: 13-15 Wilson).

The Rig Veda says that Indra ordered Maruts to proceed and fight with Krishna.

These lines of Rig Veda's sukta no 96 of the Ashtam Mandala refers to some ancient legend involving Indra and Krishna. It is interesting to note that here Krishna is referred to as Asura. Though Mahabharata and Puranas continue to underline the animosity between Indra and Krishna scholars reject the idea that Asura Krishna of Rig Veda and Vasudeva Krishna of the Mahabharata were one and the same.

Again in the same Ashtama Mandala of the Rig Veda sage named Rishi Krishna is mentioned as composer of Suktas 85-87 dedicated to Ashvini Kumars. He is seen here propitiating the twin gods by offering them delightful Soma drink. He has no link with Vasudeva Krishna of the Mahabharata.

In the Chandogya Upanishada, ascribed to seventh century B.C., there is a mention of one Krishna Devakiputra disciple of Ghora Angirasa. Krishna Vasudeva too was son of Devaki and there is lot of similarity between the teachings of Ghora Angirasa and Gita. This led many scholars to conclude that both were the same. But the possibility seems to be remote as nowhere in puranic literature we find the name of Ghora Angirasa as teacher of Vasudeva Krishna.

Panini, author of the work of grammer called Ashtadyayi, ascribed to sixth century B.C., in a Sutra Vasudevarjunabhyam Vun (IV. 3.98) extols the divinity of Krishna and Arjuna. This means he was knowing the story of Krishnarjuna and Mahabharata war.

Buddhist Jataka stories are ascribed to the time of Buddha or even earlier., anterior to 600 B.C. Later number of them artistically engraved on the stone railings and torana, gates of Buddhist stupas such as those found at Sanchi, Bharhut, Anaravati and also painted on the walls of Ajantha caves.

A very interesting version of Krishna legend is found narrated in one of the Buddhist Jataka tales. In the Ghata Jataka Krishna is described as a son of Devagarbha and Upasagara. Here in no uncertain terms identity of Krishna is very clear. Episodes like killing of Kansa and his two wrestlers, Chanur and Mushtik, and final annihilation of Vrishni clan too finds mention in it, though with some difference. Krishna's unique and formidable weapon, the Chakra, too is mentioned here along with his another name, Keshava.

The exact time of composition of nucleus of Mahabharata by Vyasa is not known. Scholars point out that in an inscription of 445 A.D. there is a reference to Samhita of

Vedavyasa. In Vajrasuchi Upanishada of Kanishka' court poet Ashvaghosha we find verses from Harivamsha and Mahabharata. On this basis the scholars contend that Mahabharata must have been older than 600 B.C. and must have been composed before the advent of Buddha. (Sanskrit Vangmaya Kosha, Varnekar, Grantha Khanda, 259).

This may mean that reference to Krishnarjuna in Panini and Krishna story in Jataka might have been taken from the Mahabharata itself.

The Mahabharata grew in three stages - Jaya, Bharata and Mahabharata over centuries. It acquired it's present form sometimes between 200 to 400 A.D., according to one opinion. It's grown form merely eight thousand verses to more than one Lakh verses was phenomenal. Maurice Winternitz wrote: 'In reality one can speak of Mahabharata as an epic and as a poem in a very restricted sence. Indeed, in a certain sense, Mahabharata is not at all a poetic product but rather an entire literature.'

The story and the character of Krishna must have grown in proportion. We do not have a clue as to how Vyasa portrayed Krishna in his original version, Jaya, and after that which additional material went into his making in subsequent editions.

However we have some clues from other sources about the growth of his cult and influence.

For instance, as pointed out by R.G. Bhandarkar in his book Vaishnavism Shaivism and Minor Religious systems, Niddesha, one of the books of Pali Buddhistic canon ascribed to fourth century B.C., speaks of contemporary religious systems and superstitions. Among different cults, some of them worshippers of animals, it had mentioned the cults of Vasudeva and Baladeva.

Megasthenes, the envoy of Greek king Seleucus Nicator to the court of Magadha emperor Chandragupta Maurya, ascribed to fourth century B.C., in his work Indika exhibits the knowledge of river Yamuna, the cities of Mathura and Krishnapura and flourishing cult of Indian Herakles, Krishna, in the Surasena region.

In the third Adhyaya of 14th Adhikarana of Kautilya's Arthashastra, ascribed to fourth century B.C., both Krishna and Kamsa are invoked in the context of success of mantra-prayoga to make dogs go to sleep in the night till morning so that the mantrik can accomplish his task during that time. Along with several others they are described as shatamayam or ones who knew hundred kinds of esoteric magic. The book also mentions Balarama and his cult members in the third Adhyaya of 13th Adhikarana.

There are certain inscriptions which give us clue to the popularity of Krishna cult in the second century B.C.

Dion's son Heliodorus, Greek ambassador to the court of Shunga king Kustiputra Bhagabhadra erected a Garuda pillar at Vidisha in Central India in about 126 B.C. in the honour of Vasudeva-Krishna proclaiming himself to be a follower of Bhagavata cult. The Brahmi inscription on the pillar reads:

1. (De)va Devas Va(sude)vas Garudadhwaje Ayam
2. Karite (Ea) Heliodorena Bhaga—
3. vatena Dias Putrena Takkasilakena
4. Yonadutena agatena maharajasa
5. Amtalikitasa up(m)ta sakesa(m) rano

Text B'

1. Trini amutapadani.......(pta)
   anu thi tani
2. nayamti svaga(m) damo chago apramado.

In this inscription Vasudeva-Krishna is described as God of gods, supreme deity and extolled the virtues such as self control (damo), self-denial (chago) and watchfulness (apramado). The virtues mentioned in the text B are imbibed in the Mahabharata. That means the epic was fairly known at the time. Garuda pillars were built in front of temples. The presence of Vidisha Garuda pillar indicates that once upon a time there was a temple of Vasudeva - Krishna in front of it.

This shows that during this period temples were built in the honour of Vasudeva-Krishna. This again is confirmed by an inscription of 100 B.C. (200 B.C. according to some) found at Ghosundi near Nagari in Chittorgarh district of Rajasthan. It speaks of stone wall constructed around the temple of Samkarshana and Vasudeva known as Narayana vataka. Thus reads the inscription

1. (Karito ayam Radnya Bhagava) (te)na Gajayanena Parashari—putrena Sa
2. Vartatina Ashvamedha-Ya Jina

   Bhagava (da*) bhya Sankarshana—Vasudevabhyam
3. (Anihatabhyam Sarveshvara) bhyam Puja-shila prakaro Narayana vataka

In this inscription king Sarvatata calls himself Bhagavata, devotee of Krishna. Suvira Jaiswal informs that 'archaeological excavations have brought to light a rectangular stone enclosure at a place known as Hathibada. The site contains walls nearly ten feet high and appears to have been place of worship mentioned in the inscription. It is evident that Nagari, identified with the ancient city of Madhyamika, contains shrines not only of Sankarshana and Vasudeva but also of Narayana after whom the site was named.' (The Origin and Development of Vaishnavism, p. 191).

Naneghat cave inscription (near Pune in Maharashtra) of Satavahana queen Nayanika, ascribed to second century B.C.) 'opens with the adoration to Sankarshana and Vasudeva along with Indra, Prajapati and the deities of four quarters Yama, Varuna, Kubera and Vasava. This certainly indicates the prime position the two gods enjoyed. (Epigraphia Indica, Vol. X, App., p. 121.)

Apart from these inscriptions of second century B.C. we know of coins depicting the likeness of Krishna and Balarama, belonging to the same century. It is interesting to note that earliest representation of Krishna and Balarama is found on the bronze coins of Greek king Agathocles (c. 180-165 B.C.) who along with his brother, Pantaleon, ruled from Taxila over quite a large portion of Indian territory extending into eastern Punjab. The diadem wearing Krishna on the coin is holding a circular disk-like weapon, chakra, in one hand and conch in another. Balarama is depicted on the coin as carrying his mace and plough.

As far as Krishna sculptures are concerned, quoting Curtis Dr. D.C. Sirkar says that an image of Herakles (i.e. Vasudeva Krishna) was being carried in front of the Paurava army, as it advanced against the Greeks led by Alexander the Great. (The Cultural History of India, Vol. IV, p. 115). However we have not found any Krishna image of that period.

An inscription recovered from a well in Mora, a village near Mathura and ascribed to first century A.D. 'records the setting up of the statues of the holy five heroes (Bhagavatam Panchaviranam' of the Vrishnis in a stone temple (shiladevagrihe) built be a woman named Tosa. The images made of stone were meant for worship and are said to have a glowing and exceedingly handsome appearance.' (Luders, EI XXIV, p. 199f). J.N. Banerjee identifies them as Baladeva,Vasudeva, Samba Pradyumna and Aniruddha.

However, an interesting terracotta plaque showing Vasudeva carrying Krishna over his head across flooded Yamuna, ascribed to first century A.D. is housed in Mathura Museum. It is a first known representation of a Krishna story.

N.P. Joshi in his Bharatiya Murtishastra says that the tradition of sculpting on stone the Krishnalila scenes dates back to Kushana period or even earlier.

As for as dramatic representation of Krishna story is concerned we find that since ancient times dance, drama, music formed the part of ritual worship of Krishna. Grammarian Patanjali, ascribed to 150 century B.C. states in his Mahabhashya that the temples of Balrama, Keshava and Kubera used to reverberate with music - mridangashankha tunavah prathannadanti samadi prasade Dhanapati-Rama-Keshavanam.

But more than this Patanjali refers to manner in which saubhikas (actors), chitras (artists through paintings) and granthikas (bards) represent the story of Kansa Vadha. Obviously actors must have been dramatising Krishna story, artists painting it and narrator Granthikas or bards singing it. It means during second century B.C. we start finding paintings of Krishna, dramatic enactment of his legends and also recitation of his stories.

Chronology is a great problem of Indological studies. Playwright Bhasa is differently ascribed to fourth century B.C. to third century A.D. He wrote number of plays depicting mythology of Krishna like Dutavakyam, Balacharitarn, and plays based on Mahabharata legends such as Madhyama Vyayoga, Karnabharam, Dutaghatotkacha, Urubhangam. He not only identifies Krishna as an incarnation of Vishnu but mentions a few more incarnations of the same deity such as Narasimha,Vamana and Ramachandra and refers to Narayana frequently.

During the period of evolution of Mahabharata, our other sources informs us that in the fourth century B.C. the cult of Krishna started picking up with Mathura as its centre. In the second century B.C. the inscriptions tell us that temples were built in his honour and even Greeks became followers of Bhagavata religion. Various art forms such as painting, drama, music picked up themes from Krishna story and recognised Vishnu's other incarnations.

Probably at this point of time need was felt to know earlier life of Krishna which did not find much scope in the Mahabharata. To fill in this lacuna Puranas like Harivamsha, Bhagavata were written. Other Puranas such as Vishnu, Brahmavaivarta, etc. carried legends of Krishna. Several works of poetry in Sanskrit and regional languages came up in subsequent centuries. There was a huge expansion of Krishna legend and so many colours were added to his personality as we find in the Mahabharata so much so that he started looking more and more as Gopala Krishna, Gopi Krishna and Radhe Krishna, Ras overshadowing Gita, madhurya of Gokul-Vrindavana obscuring aishvarya of Dwaraka-Indraprashtha.

In the Mahabharata for the first time Krishna appears at the end of Adiparva on the occasion of Swayamvara of Draupadi, daughter of Panchalanaresha Drupada, in his capital. At that time he was prince of Dwaraka. He recognised the Pandavas who were attending the Swayamvara in disguise. Arjuna won the Swayamvara and Draupadi became wife of five brothers. Krishna and Balarama went to see Pandavas where they were staying and introduced themselves. After that they left for Dwaraka. That was the beginning of friendship of Pandavas and Krishna.

Krishna help Pandavas in creating their capital Indraprastha on the bank of river Yamuna. Once on the occasion of festival at Raivataka mountain Arjuna saw beautiful sister of Krishna, named Subhadra. With the connivance of Krishna he ran away with her and married her.

When Yudhisthira decided to perform Rajasuya Krishna helped him. He told Pandavas that it was necessary to kill Jarasandha, emperor of Magadha, as he could create problem in successful completion of the Yajna. At that time

Krishna told them about his killing Kansa, king of Mathura, son-in-law of Jarasandha, and his invasion of Mathura. With the help of Bhima Krishna eleminated Jarasandha. It indeed was a great achievement considering political situation of the country.

Rajasuya Yajna was a grand affair which left Kauravas, cousins of Pandavas ruling from Hastinapur, extremely jealous. Through it the ruling kings recognised the emergence of Pandavas as a political force. The honour of Agrapuja was given to Krishna recognising his position in the royal dynasties. This established the superiority of Krishna among the royalties. When Shishupala, king of Chedi, objected the choice of Krishna for the honour, Krishna killed him.

In the Sabha Parva while supporting the idea of offering Agrapuja to Krishna, Bhishma narrated his earlier life he spent in Braj region in details including killing of Kamsa and defeating Jarasandha, then shifting to Dwaraka. Bhishma narrated entire career of Krishna and his exploits in full. Including his divine origin.

Krishna left Pandavas at the hight of glory but due to foolishness of Yudhisthira they lost everything to Kauravas in a game of dice. They were exiled for twelve years. Krishna could do little to save the situation as he was away.

However when Pandavas lost their beautiful wife Draupadi in game of dice, winner Kauravas tried to disrobe her. That time Krishna ran to her rescue and remaining invisible he covered her with yards and yards of cloth.

There is a beautiful folk tale highlighting the relationship of Draupadi and Krishna. Says the legend once Krishna cut his fingers and they started bleeding. His queens started running around in search of a piece of cloth to bandage his fingers. But in the royal palace of Dwaraka they could not find a small piece of cloth. When Draupadi heard about this she immediately tore her very precious saree and with a peace of cloth thus procured she bandaged the fingers of Krishna. The legend says that to repay the debt of Draupadi who gave Krishna a small piece of her own garment Krishna provided Draupadi with yards and yards of cloth to cover her body.

Divinity of Krishna is again and again stressed in the Mahabharata on several occasion and described him as an incarnation of Narayana and Vishnu.

Krishna continued to occasionally visit Pandavas during their period of exile. One day sage Durvasa along with his several disciples appeared before Pandavas when they were resting after taking their food. However, Yudhisthir invited them for meals. Accepting their invitation Rishi Durvasa went for ritual bath on the river, assuring Pandavas that they would return soon for food.

Draupadi had no food in her hut. She was blessed by a magic pot by the grace of Sun god, Surya. It used to produce food till Draupadi had her meals. That day unfortunately Draupadi had her meals and thus it was out of question for her to get food from magic pot given to her by Surya.

She prayed Krishna requesting him to save her from this difficult situation.

To her surprise she saw Krishna himself standing at her door. He was looking tired and famished. He told Draupadi that he was very hungry and immediately needed something to eat.

Draupadi was terribly embrassed by the request of her brother. She pleaded helplessness as she had already taken her meals and cleaned the magic pot given to her by Sun.

But Krishna insisted and wanted to see the magic pot himself. When Draupadi brought it to him he found a very small piece of vegitable sticking inside the magic pot. With great relish Krishna picked it up and put it in his mouth.

Pleased by this frugal meal Krishna said that his stomach is full and hunger gonc.

Being universal soul, vishvatma, when he said that his belly was full the hunger of all the living being became satiated. So felt sage Durvasa and his ten thousand disciples also who were taking ritual bath in the river. 'We are feeling so full that now it is impossible for us to eat anything' told the disciples to their Guru who too had same feeling.

Durvasa thought that if they would not take food at Pandava's residence they would be very angry. Thinking this he ran away with his disciples to escape from the wrath of their hosts.

After completing the years of exile as per the condition the Pandavas emerged on the scene and started demanding their share of kingdom. They knew that Kauravas would not relent easily so they started preparing for war. The idea of conflict did not appeal to Krishna. He went to Kaurava court with the message of peace but his conciliatory efforts failed.

And then ensued great Bharata war in which nearly half of Kshatriya race perished. Krishna did not actively participated in the war but remained as main counselor of Pandavas. He became charioteer of Arjuna led Pandavas to victory. Pandavas fought bravely but entire stategy was chalked by Krishna, hence the adage-Yato Krishna tato jaya:

Krishna narrated Gita right on the battlefield to Arjuna to make him act and taught him philosophy of selfless action or Karma. It was the basically essence of Upanishadas. Gita was not just a verbal discourse, If we look at Krishna's life we would realise that he told as he lived. Gita may be described as the ideological biography of Krishna. Krishna and Gita are reflections of one another.

Krishna's end was tragic. He witnessed the terrible scene of Yadavas in killing each other in fratricidal conflict under the influence of liquor. His end came when he was hit by an arrow of a hunter when he was standing under a tree in a Yogic posture. It was an end of an era.

Mahabharata describes Aishvarya phase of Krishna, later Puranas and poetic literature his Madhurya Phase. However Mahabharata throughout upheld his divine status and referred to him as an incarnation of Narayana Vishnu. And indeed by his actions he rose to that unique status.

While speaking about Krishna in the Adiparva Bhishma has referred to his many adventured right from his childhood including killing of several demons including Putana, subduing serpent Kalia, lifting up of mountain Govardhana, subduing Indra, killing of Kansa, bringing back to life the son of his teacher Sandipani, defeating Jarasandha and leaving Mathura establishing the city of Dwaraka.

While in Dwaraka he led a military expedition against Bhumiputra Narakasura, also known as Bhaumasura, of Pragjoyotishpur to relieve the ear-rings of goddess Aditi stolen by him and killed him.

Naraka's story is found in bits in the epics and Puranas but full length portrait of this king is given in the Kalika Purana. In the copper plate land grants of the early Hindu kings of Kamarupa who ruled from 7th to 12th century A.D. we find references to Naraka claiming him to be their remote ancestor. It seems that mythical Naraka and Historical Naraka got mixed up. It is believed that it was Naraka who encouraged local shakti cult of Kamakhya.

In the Mahabharata it is said that Narakasur used to live underground near Murtilinga. This may mean, image in form of linga, may be female one. This could be a reference to underground Kamakhya linga.

An ardent devotee of Shiva, king Banasura was a ruler of Shonitpura. His beautiful daughter Usha fell in love with Aniruddha, son of Pradyumna. They both started living in the royal palace of Shonitpura. When Bana came to know about this he captured Aniruddha and threw him in prison. Krishna attacked Bana, defeated Lord Shiva and Bana himself and freed Aniruddha. Krishna frightened Rukmi and by defeating him kidnapped Rukmini. He defeated king of serpents, Vasuki, by attacking his capital Bhogapuri. These were some of the prominent adventures of Krishna described by Bhishma.

The stories of Krishna's marriages, mostly with beautiful princesses of royal families, are full of advanture and romance. Different Puranas had different lists of names. However the Bhagavata mentions the names of Rukmini, Satyabhama, Kalindi, Mitravinda, Satya, Bhadra, Kaikeyi and Lakshmana. Most significant name mentioned in other Puranas, but missing in the Bhagavata, is of Jambavati, daughter of Jambavan.

The story of Krishna's marriage with princess Rukmini, daughter of King Bhishmaka of Vidarbha, with his capital at Kundinpur is very famous. Rukmini desired Krishna but her brother Rukmi wanted her to marry his friend prince Shishupala. Rukmini secretly wrote a love letter to Krishna which was delivered to him by her Brahmin messanger. Krishna rushed to Kundinpur, when he saw Rukmini coming out of the temple of goddess Amba he lifted her up on his chariot and swiftly started moving towards Dwaraka. When the kings assembled to attend the Rukmini Swayamvar led by Rukmi attacked Krishna he defeated them and took his bride to Dwaraka.

Satya was daughter of king Nagnajita of Kosala. Krishna won her in Swayamvara by subduing seven strong bulls in one go. He got Jambavati when he defeated her father Jambavan for wrestling with him for twentyeight days. He won Lakshmana, daughter of Madra king, in swayamvara. Same was the case of Bhadra who was daughter of Kekayadhipati Ghrustaketi. Satyabhama was daughter of Yadava king Satrajita. Satyabhama was very beautiful. She was extremely jealous of Rukmini and the stories about their rivalry are found in folk poetry and drama. Bhamakalapam is very well known opera of Kuchipudi school of dance-drama.

It is said that when Krishna rescued 16 thousand beautiful princesses kept captive by Narakasura they married him.

Krishna mythology in the Mahabharata is very vast. Basically we see him in the epic as astute statesman and warrior hero. This phase of his life is described as Aishvarya phase. Madhurya or sweetness of his career is more evident in his childhood lilas described by Puranas, more sweetly so by Bhagavata.

Lila or play is intrinsic part of the divine. David R. Kinsley had studied this aspect of divine in his book The Divine Player. He writes: 'play as a divine activity in India is nowhere more fully illustrated than in the god Krishna. Among Indian gods he is certainly the most playful. His sport is more diverse, more sustained than the play of any of the deities, (p. 56)

Vrindavan on the bank of river Yamuna is considered as 'playground of Krishna', the place where his Bal lilas or childhood sports manifested beautifully. Devotees prefer Vrindavan Krishna to Mahabharata Krishna. Even in the Mahabharata when Krishna showed Arjuna his universal form having tremendous grandeur, Vishvarupa, Arjuna pleaded with him to assume his pleasing form as he could not bear the divine majesty of the Lord which was quite frightening.

Gradually the cult of Krishna evolved into cult of joy with Bal lila or childhood frolics, he performed in the beautiful region of pastoral Braj on the bank of river Yamuna, at its centre. Expericing Krishna, says Bhagavata Purana, is experiencing pure bliss - kevalanibhavanan-daswarupa. He filled the hearts of residents of Braja with joy by his sweet childhood pranks—vrajasyovah vai harsham bhagavan balachestieh.

Bhagavata Purana has described extensively pleasure—giving blissful Bal lila of Krishna. Both Balarama and Krishna gleefully played with lovely birds and animals of pastoral Braj such as deers, peacocks, cows. They were particularly fond of monkies. As they grew they came to be known as butter thieves or makhan chor. They would enter the huts of cowherd girls, steal milk and curd and distribute among monkies.

One day child Krishna consumed mud and his naughty friends told this to mother Yshoda. When angry mother rebuked him he refused that he has swolled it. When mother asked him to open his mouth with great persuation he opened it. And lo: mother Yashoda saw entire universe moving in his open mouth.

One day angry due to his pranks mother Yashoda tied him with rope to a mortar. Krishna dragged the mortal in the courtyard where two tall Arjuna trees stood majestically close to each other. Krishna tried to pass through it but the passage was very narrow but that did not deter his onward march. When mortar struck between the trees he applied tremendous force. By his action the great trees were uprooted. In fact the trees were sons of Kubera, treasurer of gods who had turned into the trees due to the curse of divine sage Narada.

Number of demons he and his brother Balarama killed in the Braj are mentioned in the Mahabharata's Adiparva itself. But most famous acts of Krishna described with relish by Bhagavata is killing of demoness Putana, subduing serpent Kalia and lifting of mountain Govardhana.

Putana was a cruel demoness fond of killing children. Once she assumed the form of very beautiful woman and entered the house of Nanda in Gokula. She lifted infant Krishna and tried to feed him by placing in his mouth her breast smeared with deadly poison. Krishna sucked her breast with such a force that she started trembling with fright, and started crying loudly for help. She could not withstand the might of Krishna sucking at her breast and she lost her life.

Serpent Kalia used to live in river Yamuna along with his family. Their poisonous breating contaminated the environment of Braj region. Krishna forced him to leave Yamuna and migrate to sea.

It was a tradition of cowherd community of Braj to celebrate the festival of Indra and worship him annually. But Krishna negated the idea of performing Indra-yaga and instead suggested that they should worship mountain Govardhana instead. Angered by Krishna's suggestion and subsequent worship of Govardhana by cowherd community of Braj, Indra, god of thunder and shower, lashed Braj with rains and storm for seven days. Krishna lifted the mountain Govardhana and gave shelter to the people of Braj till the fury of thunder shower ended.

However the most significant lila of Krishna in Braj was Ras dance he performed on the bank of river Yamuna with cowherd girls, fair as Champak flowers, on the full-moon day of Sharad ritu. Ras is not mentioned in the Mahabharata but subsequent Puranas such as Harivamsha, Vishnu, Bhagavata and Brahmavaivarta. Except of Brahmavaivarta which was probably composed in 16th century no other Puranas mentioned above take the name of Radha.

The five chapters in the Bhagavata Purana known as Rasa Panchadhyayi are very lyrical and full of titillating romance.

After killing Kamsa the tyrannical ruler of Mathura and fighting many battles with his father-in-law Emperor Jarasandha of Magadha he shifted to Dwaraka, a city he created on the western sea-shore.

In the later literature, particularly that flourished in the Braj region in the local language Krishna became the presiding deity of naughty and colourful festival of Holi. We got beautiful description of Radha playing Holi with Krishna in Garga Sahita, a Sanskrit work of uncertain date.

The book says once friends of Radha told her that Krishna has come to her locality with his friends to play Holi. She came out of her palace with her female friends and encircled Krishna singing Holi songs and teasing him by giving 'galis' in humorous mood. Every year the festival of Holi is celebrated with lot of fun and frolic. There are various local customs which villages observe during fortydays of biosterous celebration. Rangili Holi of Barasana which is also known as Lathamar Holi, fire ordeal of Phalen, rolliking Holi of Baldeogaon enlivens the festivity. Songs, drama, music programmes are organised and Raslila theatre regales the devotees.

Vrindavan-Krishna is an epitome of bliss, the Rasa. His eternal companion Radha is termed as his Hladini Shakti or bliss generating potency. Another companion of Krishna, like Radha, is his flute, a simple musical instrument made of bamboo reed which spells magic. Krishna is an infinite joy incarnate and all his lilas or sports spring from this basic nature of his and hence they are blissful.

Krishna partook this blissful nature from Vishnu whose incarnation he was. Harivamsha and Vishnu Puranas speak of Hari sleeping in primordial waters and in delightful mood, playful to the core, enjoys himself. Referring to this David R. Kinsley in his book. The Divine player (p. 3) states: The Harivansha also refers to the image of Vishnu playing in the primordial waters. Thereupon, for purpose of creating creatures the 'Eternal Hari lay in the great ocean and sporting in diverse ways, attained to great delight. And Vishnu Purana also pictures Vishnu as sporting boy. 'Vishnu being thus discreate and indiscreate substance, spirit and time, sports like a playful boy.' (I.2.18; Vishnu Purana, trans. H.H. Wilson, p. 9).

Vishnu Purana defines the lila of Vishnu as Balakasya Krida or sport of playful child. This aspect of Vishnu is reflected in the childhood sports of boy Krishna of Vrindavan. Vishnu had no childhood so he took incarnation as Krishna.

Radha, beautiful cowherd girl of Braj, was a mysterious but lovely addition to Krishna lore. She is not found mentioned in prominent works narrating the life of Krishna such as Mahabharata, Harivansha, Vishnu or Bhagavata Puranas.

For the first time we find her mentioned in a Gatha, verse, in a poetic collection named Gatha Saptashati by Hal Satavahana of Prathisthana in Maharshtra ascribed to first century A.D. In the verse she is not more than a play mate or most favourite cowherd girl of Braj.

Interestingly there is yet another verse which refers to Nipuna Gopi who kissed her female companion dancing with Krishna. Her face was full of drops of perspiration in which floted reflected images of Krishna. By kissing her face the Nipuna Gopi earned the pleasure of kissing several Krishnas. In the Ras episode of Vishnu Purana too there is a mention of a Nipuna Gopi, who on the pretext of appreciating the singing skill of Krishna, embraced and kissed him. In the very next verse there is a mention of drops of perspiration on the cheeks of cowherd girls. In Vishnu Purana and Gatha Saptashati verse similar ideas were expressed in different poetic idioms.

Mention of Krishna in Maharashtri folk verses is not surprising. Naneghat inscription of Satavahana queen Nayanika, ascribed to second century B.C. opens with invocation to Sankarshana and Vasudeva. Some scolars like S.A. Jogalekar believes that there were Abhir settlements in Maharashtra around Nasik since Satavahana times. Krishna's relationship with cowherd Abhiras is well known. Radha-Krishna love lore might have been part of Abhira tradition of Maharashtra which might have entered into Maharashtri Prakrit folk poetry.

Whatever may be the case one fact is certain that Radha for the first time as a love interest of Krishna appeared in Maharshtra around first century A.D. In the verse describing her there is no reference to her divinity. She seemed to be a simple cowherd girl, not a divinity.

But soon she acquired the divine stature. In the Panchatantra, a book of tales ascribed to fifth century A.D. she is referred as a wife of Vishnu born in a cowherd family by name Radha. Vishnu's wife is Lakshmi. By inference

Radha was considered here as Lakshmi herself. In the Devi Bhagavata, ascribed to sixth century A.D., she is described as Mula Prakriti and presiding deity of Shaktipitha of Vrindavan.

Jayadeva's Gita Govinda, ascribed to 12th century A.D., describes Radha as an intense, passionate love companion of Krishna indulging in rati-keli or amorous sports. Miller writes: 'Names of Krishna's divine consort, such as Sri, Padmavati, Kamala, Padma, Lakshmi occur to place Radha in a appropriate cosmic context. Gita Govinda despite of its highly erotic content achieved the status of a scripture and by a royal decree of king Prataprudradeva dated July 1499 Gita Govinda became the part of daily ritual service of Lord Jagannatha.

Though there are shrines of Lakshmi and Vimala in the premises of Jagannatha temple Radha shrine is conspicuous by its absence. Devi Bhagavata says that Radha and Vimala emerged out of Shakti of Krishna. Vimala is considered as tantric deity. However in poetry Radha is associated with Lord Jagannatha, he being the Krishna himself. It is believed that Radha and Krishna together live in the idol of Jagannatha Purushottama. G.N. Mahapatra in his book Jagannatha in Religion and Religious Traditions of Orissa says:

'In the eighth century when Purushottama Mahatmya of Skanda Purana was composed, Sri Jagannatha was conceived as Vishnu-Krishna and Krishna-Vasudeva but never as Krishna pious lover of Sriradha. In the nineth century however some narrowly believe in a traditional way that Shankaracharya depicted him in that way composing the line Mudabhirinaribadana kamalaswadu-madhupa. On this tradition Jayadeva in the twelfth century depicted him as Krishna, the so called husband of Radha, and Jagannatha finally became the Krishna of celebrated work, Gitagovindam. This Radhakrishna conception took a complete shape when in the 16th century at the time of

Prataprudradeva Jagannatha was visualised as the embodiment of both Radha and Krishna.' (p. 46-7)

The cult of Radha-Krishna love took many forms in Orissa and Bengal in medieval period. Under Sena rulers of Bengal this cult gradually shot into prominence culminating into Jayadeva's Gita Govinda. It evolved into Vaishnava Sahajiya cult on the model of Buddhist Sahajiyas preceeding it. Chandidasa of 14th century made Vaishnava Sahajiya movement popular followed by Vidyapati of Mithila.As explained by Shashibhushan Dasgupta all men and women were thought of as physical manifestation of the principles of Radha and Krishna, so the highest state of union of the two, which is the state of supreme love, is the final state of Sahaja.

People belived that Chaitanya Mahaprabhu was an incarnation of Jagannatha-Krishna and like in his idol at Puri temple Radha and Krishna jointly lived in his physical body.

Chaitanya visited Braj region in 16th century and his disciples stayed back. With them came to the region flavour of Gaudiya and allied Vaishnava sects of Orissa and Bengal.

A cult is a system of religious beliefs with excessive admiration for a person or a concept. When an idea of love between a divine couple Radha and Krishna became the focal point of religious system we call it a cult of love. In the 16th century Vrindavana a number of love cults with Radha and Krishna as their presiding icons emerged and were collectively known as Rasika Sampradayas. They evolved the idea of Nikunja lila and Nitya Vihar.

According to this concept in the lovely woods and bowers on the bank of river Yamuna the love making of Radha and Krishna is going on perennially without stop. The devotee peeps through the bowers and derive the spiritual pleasure watching amorous sports of the divine couple.

All this is conceived on mental level. Devotee mediates upon the whose scene of amorous sports and no corresponding physical ritual or action is involved, like tantras.

However in Vraj region Radha gained supreme importance in some cults, like Radha Vallabh sect of Hita Harivamsha 'with whom the blessed feet of Radha were the highest object of worship. In his work Chaurasi Pada Hita Harivamsha has written about romantic dalliance and amorous sports of Radha Krishna's Nikunja lila. In one of his poems he says:

'At day-break the wanton pair, crowned with victory in love's conflict were all exuberant. On her face are frequent beads of labour's dew, and all the adornments of her person are in disarray, the paint-spot on her brow is all but effaced by heat and the struggling curls upon her lotus face resembles roaming bees. Rejoice Hita Harivamsha: her eyes are red with love's colours and her voice and lions feeble and relaxed: '(Tr. F.S. Growse). Mathura a District memoir.

Radha is considered as Hladini Shakti or bliss-giving potency of Krishna. Her divine lilas are elaborately described in Brahmavaivarta Purana. Earliest known sculpture showing Radha and Krishna was found at Paharpur and was ascribed to 6th century A.D. At Barasana in Braj region of Uttar Pradesh there is a magnificent temple of Sri Radha and in her honour Latha Mar Holi is organised every year. She is profusely depicted in various schools of miniature paintings of late medieval period. Puranas and folk poets had weaved thick cluster of legends around her but basically she remained as a beloved of Krishna, divine or othervise.

11

BUDDHA

Buddha is a surprise inclusion in Avatars pantheon of Bhagavatas or one may say not so surprising entry in it. Because Buddhism and Bhagavata religion came closer together and influenced each other. Bhagavata religion or Narayaniya Dharma was influenced by the tenet of Ahimsa, non-violence, of the Buddhist creed. Jayadeva in his Gita Govinḍa describing the Buddha incarnation stated :

Kind hearted Gautama
condemned Vedic rituals stipulating
animal sacrifice

O Keshava, assumer of the form of Buddha

Victory to you Jagadisha Hare.

A work on Natya writing about the posture of Buddha to be shown on the stage says :

Stabdha Shirsha.

At the time of Mahabharata, according to its Shanti Parva, arose a debate among gods and seers about the meaning of the word Aja in the context of ritual sacrifice. Gods told the seers that Aja means sacrificial goat. But seers differed with this interpretation. They argued that Aja does not mean animal but food grain. It is not the religion of satpurushas to sacrifice animals in the Yajna.

Mahabharata states that there was a pious king by name Uparichara Vasu who was devotee of Bhagavan Narayana. He performed Ashvamedha Yajna without sacrificing a single animal. Instead fruits and vegetable produced in the forests were offered to gods as sacrificial oblations.

This transformation was happening in the Cult of Vishnu, Narayana, Vasudeva, Hari. Gradually in the Bhagavata Dharma Yajna was replaced by Bhakti.

At the other end Upanishadic philosophy influenced Buddhism. In the 7th century A.D. Pallava king of Kanchi Mahendra Vikram Varman, wrote a farce titled Matta Vilasa Prahasana or Farce of a Drunken Monk. In this Prahasana monks of different religious systems fight among themselves to prove supremacy of their own cults. A monk belonging to Shaiva Kapalika sect tells Shakya Bhikshu that is Buddhist monk that instead of saying Namo Buddhaya you people should say Kharapataya Namh. It was Acharya Kharpat who composed a treatise on the science of thieving. Bhuddha is more expert in this field who stole material from Vedanta (Upanishadas) and Mahabharata and filled his own coffer by hoodwinking Brahmins.

In ancient times Buddha was not shown in human form. He was represented by certain symbols like Bodhi tree, empty alter, wheel of law. Gradually sculptors started making images of Buddha at Mathura and Gandhara. A art Critic wrote : 'The sculptors of Mathura undoubtedly deserved the credit of creating the earliest and entirely Indian representations of Buddha.'

A second century A.D. life size Buddha image, one of the firsts, carved at Mathura and found at Sarnath was inspired by colossal Yaksha statues of the Maurya period. Vasudevasharn Agrawala in his Bharatiya Kala writes that Bhakti Dharma, Bhagavata movement, worship of Sankarshana Vasudeva, making of images and temples for them influenced Buddhists to make images of Buddha (p. 243).

N.P. Joshi in his Bharatiya Murtishastra writes that we start getting the images of Vishnu from Kushana period. Out of 50 Vishnu images ascribed to this period 40 are from Mathura and those are inspired by Yaksha images. (p. 47)

Buddha and Vishnu images were inspired by Yaksha images initially, that too they were made in Mathura. This created similarity in the mode of their worship. Song, dance, music, drama were offered to both Vishnu and Buddha. One of the early Indian playwright was Buddhist by name Ashvaghosha. His plays were enacted in the Buddhist monasteries of Mathura.

Fa-hien says: 'Actors were hired to perform a play in which Sartiputra who was originally a Brahmin, goes to the Buddha to ask for ordination. Scenes from the lives of Maudgalyaputra and Kasyapa are also depicted in this way in Mathura.'

Presenting plays in temples based on the lilas of Hindu gods is a typical Bhagavata tradition, latter borrowed by Buddhists. And that too great opposition to dramatic arts recorded in Buddhist scriptures.

Epigraphist D.C. Sirkar writes : 'Devadasis were mentioned in early medieval period not only in Brahmanical temples but also in Buddhist shrines at least in eastern India (Ep. Ind. Vol. XXXV, No. 12, p. 97-98).

Period of Orissan history from the end of Kharvela to the emergence of Gangas and Bhumaras in the 6th century A.D. is called Buddhist period. The Buddhist community in Orissa continued to flourish upto 12th-13th centuries A.D. This gave rise to the theory that it was Buddha who was later worshipped as Jagannatha.

It may or may not be true but in the 12th century poet Jagannatha in his Dashavatara Ashtapadi has indeed addressed Jagannatha as Buddha. There are evidences to show that Buddhist relics were absorbed in Hindu fold. A huge Shiva linga housed in two storied Bhaskareshvara temple at Bhubaneshvar was originally a large part of Ashokan pillar.

Number of western scholars upheld the view that Jagannatha cult is a by product of earlier Buddhist religion that flourished in Kalinga at least since the invasion of Ashoka. It is believed that in olden days Puri on the seashore was one of the more prominent centres of Buddhism.

Puri District Gazetteer says : 'The story of Buddha's tooth-relic, as it is found in the 12th century Sinhalese work, Dathavamsa, written by one Dhammakitti Thera was once in wide circulation. It is mentioned in this story that the sacred tooth of Buddha remained for centuries at Dantapura of Kalinga. This Dantapura was identified by some as Puri..... Basing on this legend Fergusson writes that there can be little doubt but that (the temple of Jagannatha at Puri) now occupies the site where formerly stood the Dagoba containing the celebrated tooth-relic.

Sir Alexander Cunningham in his work, The Stupa of Bharhut and Bhilsa Topes, advocated the view that figures of Jagannatha, Subhadra and Balarama had been derived from the Buddhist Tri-ratna or Triple Gem Symbol signifying Buddha, Dharma and Sangha.

According to Dr. Mahatab the Savaras of Orissa were converted to Buddhism during the reign of Ashoka and worshipped the Tri-ratna symbol placed in a Buddhist Stupa at Puri. Later in the 7th or 8th century when Buddha was considered as an Avatara of Vishnu, Jagannatha was also considered to be an Avatara of Vishnu. Gradually Buddhism lost itself to Vaishnavism.' (Origin of Jagannatha Deity, J.P. Sing Deo, p. 21-22)

To explain why Buddha form was assumed by Vishnu some interesting legends were invented by the Puranas.

Explaining the rationale behind Vishnu's Buddha incarnation the Agni Purana says that once a war broke out between gods and demons, that is Daityas and Asuras, in which gods suffered defeat. They went to Lord Vishnu for succor. Vishnu assuming the form of Mayamoha, illusion and infatuation, took birth as a son of Shuddhodana. He misled the Daityas and made them relinquish Vedic religion. They became followers of Buddha and made others too leave the Vedic religion.

Then the same Mayamoha appeared as Arhat (Jain) and made other people to become Arhat. This way deprived of Vedic religion they became impious and lost their vigour.

The same legend is found in elaborate form in the Vishnu Purana. Here Vishnu as Mayamoha represents Buddhist, Jain and Charvaka philosophy and makes Asuras leave Vedic religion which led to their degradation.

Once on being defeated by Asuras the gods went to Lord Vishnu for help. They told him that now a days Asuras have started following Vedic path, they are following Varnashrama dharma and became taponishtha that is they started performing Tapa, hence they have become invincible.

From his own person Lord Vishnu created Mayamoha and assured gods that he would make daityas leave Vedic religion following which they have become powerful.

When Lord saw that Asuras were practising austerities on the bank of river he appeared before them as a nude monk with tonsured head holding peacock feathers in one of his hands. He taught them tenets of great Arhat religion and made them leave Vedic path.

Then Vishnu in Mayamoha form wore red robes and taught them Buddhist religion and made them leave pofitable Vedic religion. After that he taught them Charvaka philosophy. He said unto them :

'Can violence be a religion? It is foolish to think that by burning oblation in fire one achieves great results. Even after becoming divinity Indra has to eat shami and kashta wood he receive through Yajna an animal eating green fresh leaves is better than him. If an animal sacrificed in the Yajna goes to heaven why then the performer of Yajna kill his own father to make him reach heaven. The works extolled as Shruti has not fallen from the sky'.

By leaving Vedic religion the Asuras became weak. And when next time they fought with gods they suffered defeat.

Though Buddha was accepted in Avatara pantheon he was seldom worshipped by Brahmanical cults. The Ramayana, Mahabharata and certain Puranas such as Vayu, Vishnudharmottara do not consider Buddha as incarnation of Vishnu. Not only that some Smritis like Vriddhaharita Smriti spoke against worshipping Buddha. Writing about images of Hindu Divinities in the period A.D. 700 to 1400 N.P. Joshi states that there are no independent images of Buddha in Brahmanical art. In central and East India he is found sculpted in Dashavatar panels (Bharatiya Murtishastra, p. 107).

12

KALKI

Epics, Puranas and scriptures do not speak only about incarnations that happened in the past but also one that is going to take place in future. This future incarnation is named as Kalki, that is one going to happen in the end of age of Kali. Jayadeva in his Dashavatara Ashtapadi in Gita Govinda says :

For destroying Mlenchas pleaguing the earth

You assumed form as frightening as meteor

And become Kalki

O Keshava in Kalki form

Victory to you Jagadisha Hare

Acharya Nandikeshvara in his Abhinaya Darpana describing the symbolic hand gesture indicating Kali avatara says :

Right hand in Patak and left in Tripatak Mudra.

Kalki incarnation is described in the epics and Puranas such as Mahabharata, Kalki, Bhagavata, Brahma, Agni, Vayu, Linga, Varaha, Bhavishya and number of other Puranas.

It is said that Kalki will be born in the house of a Brahmin named Vishnu Yashas of the village Sambhal which is identified with village Shakambhari in Rajasthan. Vishnu will take this incarnation when the earth will be ruled by Mlenchas. This incarnation will appear astride a horse named Devadatta holding a sword in his hand. On the pretext of Ashvamedha Yajna he will roam around the earth killing Dasyus. After the Yajna is over he will donate all the earth conquered by him among Brahmins.

Within the span of three nights he will eliminate all the demons and contain Kali. He will kill several evil kings and herald the beginning of Krita Yuga.

Kali Purusha will leave the earth and go to Patala Loka to live with king Bali.

At the close of his Avatara he will go to forest to penance and attain Samadhi. Due to his Samadhi the great fire, Yogagni, will break out on the earth which will stand purified again. The king of this new world will be Vaivasvata Manu who would rule from Ayodhya (Prachin Charitrakosha).

Some scolars consider King Yashovarman Vishnuvardhan of Mandasor (A.D. 572-538) as the Kalki incarnation. He defeated Huna king Mihirkula and conquered the land from Brahmaputra river to Mahendra Mountain and from Himalaya to Western sea. Due to his bravery the Vayu, Matsya, Brahmana and Kalki Puranas refers to him as 'Vishnu Avatara Kalki (Prachin Charitrakosha).

Bhagavata Purana says : 'In the twilight of this age, when all kings will be thieves, the Lord of the Universe will be born as Kalki from a priest named Vishnu Yasas.' (Danielou Hindu Polytheism, p. 181).

13

OTHER MANIFESTATIONS

Satyanarayana is a form of Vishnu whose worship and Vrata is very popular among common masses. Satyanarayano Vishnu : that is Satyanarayana is none but Vishnu says Skanda Purana. The importance of Satyanarayan form of Vishnu, religious rituals associated with his worship, fruits of worshipping the deity and his legends are found mentioned in details in the Rava Khanda of Skanda Purana.

Original Skanda Purana is an ancient work but lot of extraneous material was added to it from time to time. For instance Purushottama Kshetra Mahatmya was added to it in the 14th century. Chapters related to Satyanarayana worship might have been added to it quite recently. We do not find the name of Satyanarayana mentioned in the list of Vishnu Sahastranama or in the lists of his incarnations in Puranas.

Bharatiya Sanskriti Kosha informs that there are some temples of this deity in the Himalayan region and from there his worship spread to Bengal and Maharashtra (Vol. IX, p. 627). However, the ritual worship of Satyanarayana or Satyanarayana Vrata is now known to many parts of the country including South India.

According to the legend in the Skanda Purana a poor Brahmin was living in the city named Kashipur. Seeing his miserable condition Vishnu appeared before him in the guise of a old Brahmin. He told him the importance of Satyanarayana Vrata. 'When the poor Brahmin performed that Vrata he got rid of his poverty, became rich and in due course attained Moksha, liberation from the cycle of birth and death.

Since then this Vrata became known to the people. It was performed by a wood cutter and as a result became wealthy. A king named Ulkamukha and his queen Bhadrashila were staunch devotees of Satyanarayana. From him a trader named Sadhu Vani came to know about this Vrata. Sadhu Vani vowed that he would perform this Vrata at the time of the marriage of his daughter Kalavati.

The marriage took place but Sadhu Vani forgot to worship Satyanarayana. Due to the curse of the deity he suffered terribly, he lost his business and he was thrown in the prison on the false charges of theft.

When his daughter Kalavati and wife Lilavati performed the Satyanarayana Vrata Sadhu Vani was freed from the prison and rewarded with immense wealth.

Once upon a time there was a king named Vamshadwaja. One day he saw some people of cowherd community were performing the Satyanarayan Vrata. King ignored it and even refused to accept the prasad. As a consequence his one hundred sons died and he lost his wealth and kingdom. When the repentant king himself performed the Satyanarayana Puja the pleased deity restored his wealth and kingdom and brought his sons to life.

Satyanarayana worship is performed on many auspicious occasions but generally it is performed for the welfare of newly married couple.

Nara and Narayana, two deities also famous as Rishis who performed austerities of many thousands of years in Badri in Himalayas, are according to the Adiparva of Mahabharata, were manifestations of none else but Bhagavan Vasudeva, born as sons of a deity named Dharma.

The tradition frequently mentioned in the Epic states that Arjuna and Krishna in the former birth were Nara and Narayana respectively. It seems that these two deities were quite popular at the time when Mahabharata was composed. In the very first verse of the epic obeisance is paid to them.

As a Rishi the fame of Narayana can be traced to Rig Veda. The Sukta 90 of the tenth Mandala of Rig Veda, known as Purusha Sukta, is credited to Rishi Narayana.

Suvira Jaiswal in her The Origin and Development of Vaishnavism states : 'Narayana means the place where Narah go. In other words we may say that Narayana stands for entire settlement, the collective entity of man, Nara for individual. The intrinsic and inseperable relation of Narayana with Nara, the Man, gave rise to epic myth of Nara and Narayana being constant associates and companions. (p. 35)'

Dr. R.G. Bhandarkar in his Vaishnavism Saivism and Other Minor Religious Systems states : 'The companionship (of Nara and Narayana) seems to be traceable to the Upanishad idea of two birds dwelling in a tree, friends and associates of each other. That one of those, who is called the lord and onlooker, is in the present tradition Narayana and the other, who is engaged in eating the fruit of the tree, Nara. The old idea was transferred to the new conseption of Narayana as the resting place or abode of all men. (p. 32).

Each one of them had his distinct mythology also. Particularly Narayana is having larger share of mythological literature.

Tradition considers two literay greats of India, Vyas and Valmiki, authors of the epics the Mahabharata and Ramayana respectively as Incarnations of Vishnu.

Vyas was son of fisher-woman Satyavati from sage Parashara, hence was known as Parasharya also. Satyavati's foster father Dasharaj belonged to the fisher-men community and his businness was to ferry people from one bank of Yamuna river to another. Satyavati, on becoming young, adopted the same trade.

One day Parashara Muni requested Satyavati to take him to other bank of Yamuna. Satyavati took him on her ferry boat. The fisher-woman was exceedingly beautiful and in the prime of her youth. When the boat was in mid-stream Muni Parashar, his passion aroused, asked the girl to co-habit with him.

Satyavati told him that it will not be a pleasurable experience for him as she smelt foul and carrying the odour of fish around her. Muni Parashara by his power made her a girl with sweet fragrance. Satyavati then pointed out to him that being the day time people on the both banks of river would watch them making love.

To ally her fear and sense of shame Muni Parashar created dense fog on the river bed engulfing her boat diminishing the visibility to naught. He then made love to beautiful fisher woman.

In due course Satyavati secretly gave birth to a boy on one of the islands, Dwipa, in the river. As he was born on the Dwipa he came to be known as Dwaipayana. Being of dark complexion he came to be known as Krishna. Thus he became Krishna Dwaipayana Vyas.

His literay output was simply stupendous. He edited Vedas and Puranas and also Brahmasutras. However, the most important work of Vyas was the epic Mahabharata. So stupendous and varied is this work that one scholar opined that observing the variety and richness of forms and content of this epic we can not say that it belongs to this one or that one genre of writing, in fact it is entire literature.

The epic opens with the benedictory verse in the honour of god Narayana and vows to narrate ancient tale of Vasudeva-Krishna. In the course of its narration Vyas speaks of Vishnu related divinities which form his 'avatara' pantheon. Bhagvad Gita is a part of this epic in which Vyas appears as one of the characters.

Vyasa's mother, beautiful fisher-woman Satyavati, became the wife of Kuru king Shantanu and from him got two sons—Chitrangada and Vichitraveerya. First died while fighting Gandharvas and the second by his over indulgence in amorous activities. As per convention of the time Satyavati invited Vyas to beget the heir to Kuru dynasty from two widows of Vichitraveerya. Thus were born Dhritarashtra and Pandu. Their children fought the Bharata war. Thus we may say that Vyas was responsible for sowing the seeds of great war.

Probably the story of a beautiful fisher-women who became Kuru queen was popular among people on the bank of river Yamuna. One among them, Vyas, might have picked up the thread and expanded the story of his mother to its logical conclusion. Harivamsha Purana declares Vyasa as an incarnation of Vishnu.

We know practically nothing about sage Valmiki except for a few references to him in his own epic work, the Ramayana.

In the introductory part of the epic we are told that the hermitage of Maharshi Valmiki was not far from river Tamasa. One day while taking a stroll on the bank of the river he saw a male-female pair of Krauncha birds making love to each other. Suddenly a tribal hunter appeared on the scene and shot an arrow at them killing the male Kraunch bird. A verse sprang from the mouth of kind hearted Maharshi deprecating the cruel act of the hunter. Brahma told him that the metre of the verse was suitable for composing an epic and he should narrate the story of Rama, king of Ayodhya, in this metre. Thus was born the epic Ramayana in shloka metre.

Valmiki then taught his two disciples, Lava and Kusha, who were sons of Rama living in his hermitage how to sing the epic on the accompaniment of seven stringed musical instrument called Tantri. Rama later came to be recognised as an incarnation of Vishnu.

Later an interesting legend about the early life of Valmiki was found in the Avanti Khanda of the Padma

Purana. According to this legend in his early life Valmiki was a robber by name Agnisharma. One day he way laid Saptarshis and tried to rob them. They asked him for whom he was committing this sinful act. Agnisharma told them that he was doing it for his family. The Rishis asked Agnisharma to ask his family members if they were ready to share the effects of the sins he was committing. When Agnisharma put this question to the members of his family they declined to share the fruits of his sins.

Repentant Agnisharma came back and reported the matter to Saptarshis. They asked him to perform Tapa reciting the name of Rama. For hundreds of years Agnisharma sat in the forest reciting the pious name of Rama. He was covered with the Ant-hill.

The Rishis then took him out of ant-hill, named him as Valmiki and asked him to compose an epic on the life of Rama. The final form of such legends about Valmiki is found in the Adhyatma Ramayana.

In the first Khanda of Vishnudharmottara Purana it is prophesied that in the Tretayuga Vishnu will be born as Valmiki and compose Ramayana. In the third khanda of the same Purana it is said that those desirious of earning knowledge should worship Valmiki. It also tells as to how an image of Valmiki should be made. He should be shown as an old man of fair complexion emersed in deep meditation, peaceful, nor fat nor thin of constitution. Certain community in Punjab considers Valmiki as its presiding deity.

Now-a-days Dattatreya with three heads representing the three deities Brahma, Vishnu and Mahesha and six hands is worshipped. A cow is shown standing behind him and four dogs standing in front of him. In the Puranas we do not find such a description of Dattatreya. In the Marathi scripture, Gurucharitra by Saraswati Gangadhar, ascribed to A.D. 1550 we find Dattatreya thus mentioned.

He is considered as great Yogi having supreme spiritual knowledge or Brahma Jnana. According to Brahma Purana, as per advise of his father Atri Muni, he performed penance on the bank of river Gautami (modern day Godavari) as a result of which he got Brahma Jana. The place on the bank of Godavari where he performed penance became famous as Brahmatirtha.

It is believed that Dattatreya was born on Margashirsha shuddha chaturdashi. Annual Datta Jayanti is celebrated on this day.

In the Markandeya Purana the mahatmya of Dattatreya is described in details. Once upon a time gods and demons fought a terrible war for thousands of years. Demon named Jambha was the leader of Danava army which defeated gods and became the ruler of the world.

On the advise of Brihaspati the gods went to the hermitage of Dattatreya and asked for his help. Dattatreya told them that he was defiled by the woman living with him and thus had lost his power. Gods told him that the woman he was referring to was Lakshmi herself, the mother of universe, whose company was always auspicious.

Dattatreya asked the gods to bring the demons in his presence. He would rob them of their strength by looking at them and then the gods would defeat them easily.

Heeding to the advise of Dattatreya the gods challenged demons for battle. Angry demons attacked the army of gods which ran in fright and took shelter in Dattatreya's hermitage.

Demons too reached there. When they saw beautiful Lakshmi by the side of Dattatreya they were filled with passion. They forget about persuing gods and started thinking of possessing her. Putting her in a palquin they started taking her to their abode.

Dattatreya told the gods that by their immoral behaviour the demons had lost their prowess and strength. On hearing this the gods attacked the demons and defeated them. Lakshmi returned to Dattatreya.

Markandeya Purana has projected Dattatreya as great Yogi. In this book there are number of chapters describing Dattatreya's discourse on Yoga which he taught to king Alarka.

Dattatreya, son of sage Atri and his wife Anusuya, is considered as incarnation of Vishnu in number of Puranas.

Suvira Jaiswal in her book The Origin and Development of Vaishnavism writes : 'Dattatreya appears to have been another important incarnation of Vishnu mentioned in the early lists. The Puranas represent him as a forester given to strong spirituous liquor, surrounded by women and always in the state of ecstasy. In the Markandeya Purana he is made to say that he should be worshipped with offering of meat, wine, perfumes and garlands to the accompaniment of music. Traditionally he is regarded as the author of several Tantric works, and his cult appears to have been largely Tantric. His worship is popular in Maharashtra region, and he may have been a god of some local semi-civilised tribe which was brahmanised through Vaisnavism.' (p. 145) Jaiswal's conclusion seems to be far fetched.

A legend about Shakta nature of Dattatreya is found in the Anushashna parva of the Mahabharata. Once, on the advise of Garga Muni, Haihaya king Kartiveerya Arjun went to the hermitage of Dattatreya and pleased him by his penance. However, Dattatreya told him that due to excessive drinking and womanising he has lost his power of giving blessings. However, when the king pressed him hard he granted him four boons. (Prachin Charitra Kosha, Prathama Khanda, p. 413).

According to Puranas revival of Vedas and Vedic rituals like Yajnakarma, reconstruction of Varna system and elimination of Adharma is the main objectives of his incarnation. Spread of Sanyasa dharma, aceticism, and elimination of Mlenchas are also considered as his Avatrakarya according to Puranic lore.

In the Markandeya Purana Shaktaswarupi Datta is thus described. He is seen sporting with women with a cup of wine in one of his hands. A Shakti is shown sitting on his left lap. His body is shown smeared with paste of sandalwood and a garland of fragrant flowers around his neck. Eyes red by excessive drinking he is shown enjoying the dance and music being performed by beautiful women. He loved the wine offered to him in human skull and meat offered by his devotees.

In the Vishnu Purana, in the context of the episode of Samudra Manthan, churning of ocean, there is a mention of Streerupa Vishnu or Vishnu in the form of a beautiful woman. This feminine incarnation of Vishnu is known by the name Mohini, great enchantress. Bhagavata Purana says that Daityas (demons) totally surrendered to her beauty and entrusted to her the task of distributing Amrita which emerged out of churning of ocean. She made the gods drink the Amrita.

A demon named Rahu disguising himself as god mingled among them. He drank the Amrita but his identity was revealed by Sun and Moon gods to Vishnu. Before Amrita reached his body Vishnu cut his head with Sudarshana Chakra. However, his head which had a taste of Amrita became immortal. To avenge his betrayal by the Sun and the Moon Rahu attacks them on full moon and no moon days.

When the demons came to know that they were deceived by Mohini, they fought a pitched battle with gods. After the intervention of divine sage Narada they stopped fighting.

When Shiva came to know about Vishnu assuming the form of most beautiful feminine form he requested him to appear before him in the same Mohini rupa. As desired by Shiva he appeared before him as an enchanting young beauty and started playing with ball displaying the beauty of her delicate limbs in the process. Suddenly the strong current of wind flew away her cloths exposing her beautiful and shapely body to the gaze of Shiva. Shiva lost his control and tried to make love to her.

Vishnu, then, wounded his maya, the illusion, and Shiva came to his senses.

According to Skanda Purana and Kamba Ramayana from the union of Shiva and Mohini a child named Shasta was born. In Kerala there is a sacred mountain named Sabarimala on which there is a very ancient temple of Shasta (Ayyappa).

There is a folk legend about Bhasmasura-Mohini, not to be found in Purana works. One version of it is mentioned in the Marathi scripture known as Shivalilamrita.

Once a great demon was born from the ashes smeared on the body of Shiva. He served the Lord with great devotion which pleased him. Shiva asked him to ask for any boon and the demon said that on whosoever's head he would place his hand should turn into ash. Shiva granted him the boon and named him as Bhasmasura (Bhasma = ash), or Ash Demon.

Bhasmasura wanted to know if the boon was real. He rushed towards Shiva to place his hand on his head. Out of fear Shiva ran away from his abode, Kailasa mountain.

Bhasmasura then went to Brahmaloka, the abode of Brahma. On finding him the demon ran after him to place his hand on his head. Mortally afraid of him Brahma ran towards Vaikuntha and hid behind Vishnu.

Then Bhasmasura decided to try his boon on Vishnu himself. On his way to Vaikuntha the demon saw a very beautiful woman plucking flowers in a garden. Lusitng after her Bhasmasura requested her to be his wife.

The beautiful woman Bhasmasura saw was none else but Mohini, the female form of Vishnu.

Crafty Mohini told the demon that if he would imitate her dance exactly she would marry him.

Demon agreed. Mohini started dancing showing different graceful gestures. The demon copied them easily. Mohini then as a Nritya Mudra placed her own hand on her head.

That was easy, thought the demon and placed his own hand on his own head gleefully.

As soon as the demon placed his own hand on his head, as an effect of the boon, he turned into ashes.

N.P. Joshi in his Bharatiya Murtishastra speaks about Ardhanari Vishnu known in Nepal and Kashmir as Vasudeva Kamalaja. He states that in the Basel Museum of Folk Art there is such eight armed metal image of Ardhanari Vishnu. He also refers to such images at Indreshvar temple, Panauti, Narayana Temple, Patan and Saraswati temple at Sankhu. He further informs that we start getting Ardhanari Vishnu images in Nepal since 13th century. (p. 113)

According to Matsya, Vayu and Vishnu Puranas one of the incarnation of Vishnu was known as Yajna. According to 8th skandha of Devi Bhagavata in the Swayambhuva Manvantara Adi Narayana took the incarnation as Yajna Daughter of Swayambhuva Manu, Akuti, was married to Ruchi. Yajna was born as their son. He with the help of gods saved his father from the onslaught of demons.

In the Mahabharata and Vishnudharmottara Purana one more incarnation of Vishnu, named Hansa, is mentioned. He belonged to Kritayuga. In the Adhyaya 299 of the Mokshadharma Parva of Shantiparva of Mahabharata there is a dialogue between Prajapati in the form of a Swan and one Sadhya. It is known as Hansagita. Another Hansagita is found in the 13th Adhaya of 11th Skandha of Bhagavata, verses 22 to 42. King Mandhata of Ishvaku dynasty, frequently mentioned in the Mahabharata as well as Devi Bhagavata and Padmapurana was, according to Vayu Purana, an incarnation of Vishnu.

In the Bhagavata Purana the number of incarnations is variously given as 22, 23 and 15 (see Skandha 1, chapter 3, Skandha 2, chapter 7 and Skandha 11, chapter 4).

On the magnificent sea-coast of Utkal Desha there is a sacred land of Vishnu, known as Purushottama Kshetra since ancient times. Here in a lofty temple located in the city of Puri he himself resides assuming four forms of Purushottama Jagannatha, Balabhadra, Subhadra and Sudarshana Chakra made of wood.

Work glorifying certain sacred region along with its presiding deity written by local priests is known as Sthala Mahatmya. Sthala Mahatmyas of Purushottama Kshetra are included in number of puranas such as Skanda, Brahma, Narada, Padma. Additional information is found in temple record, Madala Panji and Oṛia and Sanskrit works by locals.

In the Skanda Purana we find oldest and most elaborate account of Purushottama Jagannatha legend in its section know as Utkal Khanda or Purushottama Kshetra Mahatmya. Here is a brief account of the legend in the Skanda Purana.

In far ancient times there lived in the city of Avanti a pious king named Indradyumna. He came to know that on the mountain named Nilachala in the Purushottama Kshetra of Odra Desha there is an image of Vishnu which is worshipped by tribal Shabaras. Before he arrived at the place the image of Nilamadhava was burried due to sand storm. He reappeared in the form a sacred tree. Out of the wood of this tree four images of Bhagavan Janardan, Balabhadra, Subhadra and Sudarshana Chakra were sculpted and installed in a grand temple.

Dr. Gaya Charan Tripathi in his book Communication with God had put forward a thesis that all the four images were not installed in the temple at the same time. He writes: 'Two verses occuring in C.P. inscription of Rajarajendradeva II issued in A.D. 1198 still speak of only two deities, Purushottama and Lakshmi, in the Jagannatha temple. The first mention of the trinity of Halin (Balarama), Chakrin (Jagannatha) and Subhadra in the temple is found in an inscription engraved on the stone wall of Pataleshvara temple (situated inside the precincts of Jagannatha temple) in the year 1236 A.D.'

Skanda Purana Sthala Mahatmya mentions all the four images hence it must have been older than Pataleshvara inscription. Apart from this the Mahatmya mentions 14th century king Bhanudeva II (1307-28 A.D.). Considering this Tripathi places the Skanda Purana Sthala Mahatmya in 14th century A.D.

Tripathi further argues that 'The motif of a vanished 'original' image which is replaced by the secondary image at the wish of the Deity, is very common in the temple legends of Orissa which is introduced to explain the unusual and non-classical appearance of the most of the important Orissan icons. These icons are mostly tribal religious symbols of ancient times which have later been taken over in the Hinduism and identified with one of its important gods' (p. 9).

Tribal nature of the wooden images of Jagannatha, Balabhadra and Subhadra is very much obvious. Balabhadra image which was installed much later was fashioned after Jagannatha image. The original popular tribal religious male-female symbol was accepted as Jagannatha-Lakshmi pair at some period of time, probably because of its popularity and magico-religious significance. Archaic belief in the occult and magical powers of male-female wooden tribal symbol would have made it acceptable to the people of higher culture for their own benefit and well being. Wooden images might have been some kind of talisman used in tribal society. Probably it bestowed royal power on the worshipper. Orisan kings are seen supporting the worship of tribal cult images which were named as Jagannatha-Lakshmi by their priests. Jagannatha was later considered as monarch of Orissa and king nothing more than his representative. He ruled the state in the name of Jagannatha who might have been originally a tribal royal insignia.

Vishnu-Lakshmi cult, particularly in its Madhava (Ma means Lakshmi, Dhava is husband) was popular in Orissa. Jagannatha too was not unknown, even temple dedicated to him did exist in fifth century A.D. On this basis G.N. Mohapatra in his Jagannatha in History and Religious traditions of Orissa contends that 'we can be sure of at least this much that by the time of fifth century Jagannatha worship was there, but might not be of top importance.' (p. 33). Hence it would not have been difficult for priestly class belonging to higher culture to name the popular tribal religious symbols as Vishnu—Jagannatha and Lakshmi.

Probably when Jayadeva sung his Gita Govinda in the Jagannatha temple there were only two images of Jagannatha and Lakshmi in sanctum. Why the need was felt to introduce the image of Balarama along with these two deities?

Because gradually Jagannatha, in the popular imagination, came to be identified with Krishna. Jayadeva's Gita Govinda written in 12th century is the proof of that. Jagannatha—Krishna needed Balarama by his side who was introduced on the Vedi of the temple in early 13th century.

The tradition of making the images of Balarama, Krishna and their sister Ekanansa as a triad is as old as Kushana period (first to third century A.D.) N.P. Joshi in his book Bharatiya Murtishastra speaks of one such stone panel showing these three deities which is now in Mathura Museum. He also refers to one such sculpture showing this triad ascribed to the period of Pala king Mahipal. He also speaks of the image with this same triad housed in the Lucknow Museum (p. 105). He further says that in the triad in Jagannatha temple the central female figure is of Ekanansa though now she is known as Subhadra. The triad image of these deities are housed in Mathura Museum (three images) and Karachi Museum (one). One is located on Nand Shivalinga in Rajasthan. The image belonged to Kushana and post Kushana period.

G.N. Mohapatra in his book Jagannatha in History and Religious Tradition of Orissa reports about a bronze plaque with same triad on it ascribed to sixth or seventh century A.D. He further informs that 'there is a ruined brick temple in the village Turintara under Balipada P.S., Puri district where we find three stone images of Balabhadra, Subhadra and Krishna. This temple was buit by Baghala Devi, the queen of Aniyanka Bhima Deva II (1190-1198) and the village is still called Bagalapura after her name.

Gaya Charan Tripathi in his book Communication with God informs that the image of Ekanasha standing between Balarama and Krishna must have been common in the 6th century A.D. because Varahamihira recommends the fashioning of such images in the Brihatsamhita. The best and iconographically most perfect ancient representation of the trinity of Vasudeva-Ekanansa-Balarama in stone is found in a subsidiary temple situated within a precincts of the Lingaraja temple. The ancient trinity (A.D. 1278) of the Anantavasudeva temple, Bhubaneshvar, has of late been replaced by marble images.' (p. 385)

So we have unbroken tradition starting from Kushana period of showing Krishna, Balarama and their sister together as a triad. When Jagannatha was identified with Krishna, under the influence of triad tradition, Balarama must have been introduced in Puri temple which originally had only two images those of Jagannatha and Lakshmi. As in the triad the central female figure is of sister of Krishna, the original Lakshmi image in the Puri temple might have been recognised as Subhadra.

The triad—Krishna-Jagannatha, Subhadra and Balabhadra-placed on the Ratnavedi of Puri temple is very complex and interpreted in different ways.

As we have seen the female image identified as Subhadra is not in fact that Subhadra who was abducted by Arjuna but Ekanansa born to Nanda and Yashoda in Gokula and to whom Kansa tried to kill by banging her on the stone.

She is also called as Yogamaya, Yoganidra or Durga. Dr. Tripathi has pointed out that in Puri temple Subhadra is worshipped with mantra of Bhuvaneshvari. Bhuvaneshvari is one of the Dasha Maha Vidyas and manifestations of Durga.

Coming to Balabhadra Dr. Tripathi in his book Communication with God says : 'Balabhadra is not a totally Vaishnava deity. Though the Vasudeva mantra with which he is worshipped is the most common of all Vaishnava mantras, yet the Nyasa which seeks to lend the character of the worshipped deity to the devotee (worshipper) is the one which is used in the worship of Shiva and the presiding deity of this Nyasa, called Srikanthadi Nyasa, is Shiva in his Ardhanarishvara aspect. The analysis of the mode of worship of the three main deities (Jagannatha, Balabhadra and Subhara) of the Jagannatha temple thus shows very clearly that these three deities represent Vishnu, Shiva and Durga respectively. (p. 376)

Puri Jagannatha too was subjected to number of interpretations. Originally tribal Shabara religious symbol it was worshipped as Buddha when they came under the influence of Buddhism. He was then reclaimed as Vishnu or Nilamadhava by Hindus and interestingly Tantriks worship him as Dakshinakalika.

In the sanctum of Jagannatha temple placed on the Ratnavedi there are five wooden images of Jagannatha, Balabhadra, Subhadra, Sudarshana and Nilamadhava and two merralic images of Lakshmi and Vishvadhari.

Dr. Tripathi writes that small image of Nilamadhava was introduced much later under the South Indian influence. After Krishnaisation of Jagannatha it was substitued by a metallic image of Madanamohana or flute - playing Krishna. However the miniature statue remained in the sanctum which was popularly identified as that of Nilamadhava.

Jagannatha temple at Puri is one of the most magnificent temples of India. It was built in 12th century when Ganga dynasty was ruling over Orisa. Initially it comprised of deul or sanctury and its assembly hall or Jagamohana. Later in 14th or 15th century two more structures dancing hall or Nata Madira and hall of offering or Bhoga Mandapa were added to it.

Dance, music, drama formed important part of ritual worship and offerings to the Jagannatha. In the 8th or 9th century Murari Mishra wrote a play Anarha-Raghava in Sanskrit. It was staged on the occasion of Yatra of Jagannatha who is described in the prologue as husband of Kamala, that is laksmi.

King Chodagangadeva and his son Rajarajadeva II consecrated dancing girls, Devadasis or Maharis, to the temple. Prataparudradeva, the Gajapati ruler in his Oria inscription attached to the temple dated July 1499 ordered that dancing should be performed at Bhoga time and in the evening from Dhupa time to Bada Singar time. He also made compulsory the singing of Gita Govinda to entertain the deities.

In the 16th century Ramananda Rai worte a play named Jagannatha Vallabha and trained the Devadasis of Jagannatha temple to act in the play. Sri Chaitanya Charitamrita says that Rai used to bathe and massage the limbs of two Deva Kanyas whom he kept in his house and also do their make-up with his own hands. He taught them how to dance, express the meaning of songs through acting, express emotions and basic sentiments through eyes, facial and bodily movements. Devadasis of Puri contributed significantly to the evolution of Odissi dance.

Jagannatha dons different disguises on different occasions. Dr. Tripathi writes: 'There are some 20 different Veshas of Jagannatha which are put on him on different occasions either to commemorate some special event from the life story of Krishna (e.g. Kaliyamardana Vesha, Vanabhoja Vesha, Radhadamodara Vesha) or the legends of Vishnu (Gajoddharana Vesha, Lakshminarayana Vesha, etc.)

Sometimes they represent the different incarnations (e.g. Vamana Vesha, Nrisimha Vesha) or various aspects of Vishnu-Jagannatha (Nagarjuna Vesha, Rajadhiraja Vesha). Ganesha Vesha is the only Vesha through which Jagannatha is identified with a totally different god lying outside the pale of Vishnuism.'

Various fairs and festivals are held throughout the year to celebrate Jagannatha. Most important of them all is Ratha Yatra which is held in the month of Ashadha (June-July) when three deities-Jagannatha, Balabhadra and Subhadra—astride three different chariots are taken out in procession to Gundicha Mandir and taken back after the sojourn of a few days.

There are number of interesting legends about Jagannatha which are very popular with masses. One such legend is about 15th century Gajapati king Purushottama Deva.

Once king of Kanchi visited Puri at the time of Ratha Yatra festival to have a 'darshan' of the Lord. He was accompanied by his exquisitely beautiful daughter, princess Padmavati. King Purushottama Deva was fascinated by her charm.

During the festival, as was the tradition, the king of Orissa swept the chariot of Jagannatha with golden broom. It made poor impression on the mind of the king of Kanchi, as he saw the king of Orissa doing the job of a lowly sweeper.

When king of Kanchi returned to his kingdom Gajapati Purushottamdeva sent a marriage proposal to Kanchi king asking for the hand of his beautiful daughter. With great contempt he refused the proposal by saying that how could he give his beautiful daughter to a mere sweeper ?

Purushottama Deva felt terribly instulted as Kanchi king not only humiliated him but scoffed at the local tradition of showing utmost respect to his god.

Invoking the blessings of Jagannatha Gajapati Purushottama Deva marched against the ruler of Kanchi with huge army in tow.

Jagannatha and Balabhadra in the guise of soldiers marched way ahed of Purushottam Deva's army. On the way they felt hungry. They saw a milk-woman, Manika, who was carrying the pot of curd on her head and proceeding towards market to sell it.

The Lordships in the guise of soldiers stopped her and requested her to sell them the curd. When she asked for money Lord Jagannatha gave her his precious jem-studded gold ring and asked her to show it to Gajapati Purushottama Deva who would pay the price of the curd to her.

Manika stopped the marching king and told him that he must pay her the price of curd consumed by his two soldiers in lieu of a ring. When he saw the ring he immediately recognised it to be of Lord Jagannatha. He was over joyed to know that Jagannatha and Balarama themselves were leading his march against Kanchi.

Gajapati Purushottama Deva gave her a large sum of money and granted a village to her for her sustenance. The village came to be known as Manika Patana.

Blessed by the Lords the King of Orissa defeated Kanchi king and as a booty carried his beautiful daughter Padmavati home along with beautiful image of Ganesha. He installed this image in the premises of Jagannatha temple which is still there and is known as Kanchi Ganesha.

Gajapati Purushottama Deva handed over the princess to his Chief Minister and asked him to give her in marriage to a sweeper. Clever Chief Minister kept her in his house till the next Ratha Yatra. When, as per tradition, next year Gajapati Purushottama Deva started sweeping the chariot of the Lord with golden broom the clever Chief Minister brought the beautiful Kanchi princess before him and innocently told him that he could not find more suitable sweeper than him to marry her off.

Gajapati Purushottama Deva accepted her as his queen and suitably rewarded the Chief Minister. Historians believe the Kanchi king referred to in this story was none else but Salva Narasimha. This story is the theme of Pata Chitras of Puri.

Another legend pertains to well known 12th century Vaishnava saint of South India, Acharya Ramanuja. He visited Puri when king Chod Ganga Deva was ruling over Orissa. He did not like, it is said, the mode of worship of Jagannatha and also the association tribal Daityas with it. He powerfully argued before the king the need to introduce Puja Paddhati based on Shastric injunction. King agreed and requested the Acharya to do the needful.

Having accomplished his task Acharya went to sleep in the night thinking about the changes he would effect. But when he woke up next morning he found himself at a spot hundreds of miles away from Puri. Acharya understood that Jagannatha did not want his interference in his Puja Paddhati and his idea of removing Daityas who were favourite devotees of Jagannatha. Daitys or tribal Shabaras were real custodians of Jagannatha who make all arrangements of Ratha Yatra and perform certain rituals as temple servants.

Another important feature of the Jagannatha temple is that no caste distinctions are observed in its premises and all the devotees are treated as equals.

Orissa, particularly Bhubaneshvar region was the hub of Tantric cults like Lakulisha Pashupata and temples like Vetala Deul stands testimony to that. G.N. Mohapatra in his Jagannatha in History and Religious Traditions of Orissa writes : 'Since 8th century the Buddhist Vajrayanic Tantric aspect influenced the cult of Jagannatha for which the mode of worship of Lords contains the Pancha Makara System; while the water of green coconut was offered to the deities in bellmetal basins representing wine and so on. Due to Tantric influence Jagannatha Krishna was known as Bhairava.

Vimala Bhairavi Yatra

Jagannathastu Bhairava,

Sri Kshetre to Jagannathah,

Swayam Dakshinakalika (p. 386)

Vimala is considered as Bhairavi of Jagannatha. Animal sacrifice of goat is offered to her at her temple situated at left side of main temple on three occasions in a year.

Bhairava, a terrible form of Shiva, was considered as guardin-deity of Purushottama Kshetra and the temple. Dr. Tripathi informs that stone image of bhairava had been there on the pedestal of Jagannatha till about the end of 18th century when it was removed from the sanctum by some influential Sannyasins and destroyed. It was necessary to offer worship to Bhairava and seek his permission for offering worship to Jagannatha. (Communication with God, p. 88-93, 144).

Radha was favourite cowherd girl of Krishna during his days in Braj. For the first time she is mentioned in the Gatha Saptashati edited by Hal Satavahana around first or second century A.D. Later she was deified and was considered as Hladini Shakti, bliss giving potency, of Krishna. At least since the time of Jayadeva she got associated with Jagannatha as he was considered as Krishna. Scholars have pointed out that in the second half of the 15th century, during the rule of Purushottamadeva a mantra Gopijanavallabhacharanau Sharanam prapadye. Gopijanavallabha means 'Beloved of the Gopis or cowherd girls'. In the 16th century Chaitanya Mahaprabhu who stayed at Puri propagated the cult of Radha. We do not find her independent shrine or image in the premises of Jagannatha temple. But it is believed that Janannatha and Radha together reside in the image of Jagannatha himself.

Since Vedic times Vishnu, among his attributes, was recognised as solar deity. The Sun-god Surya is called Surya Narayana. Jagannatha being Vishnu he too assimilated the traits of solar deity, the Surya. G.N. Mohapatra in his Jagannatha in History and Religious Traditions of Orissa Writes : 'In the 13th century Narasimha Muni, a follower of Madhavacharya and then Narahari Tirtha and Jagannatha Tirtha preached Vaishnavism in Orissa. Jagannatha as their prominent deity, the temple of Jagannatha became the centre of Vaishnavism under the patronage of Ganga kings. By the time the concept of Jagannatha was merged in Sun-worship and his chariot was also called Rabi-ratha (Chariot of Sun). As a result of this prevalence of Sun worship the famous Ganga king Narasimhadeva constructed an artistic Sun temple (in the shape of chariot) at Konarka (p. 47).

In the Purushottama Mahatmya of Skanda Purana the Narasimha incarnation of Vishnu is associated with Jagannatha. There is a shrine of Narasimha in the premises of Jagannatha temple. Narasimha is invoked during Navakalevara ceremony of Jagannatha triad. It was the surmise of some scholars that once upon a time Jagannatha was worshipped by Narasimha Mantra.

In the 14th century work Yogini Tantra composed in Kamarupa-Assam there is a mention of Indradyumna legend in different version. Accordingly Vishnu appeared in the dream of king Indradyumna and instructed him to make his image out of wood of a tree on the sea shore. Indradyumna cut the tree in seven parts, out of one he sculpted an image for Odra Desha and images made out of other six parts were sent to different countries. One of them was established in Kashmir Desha as god Aditya. One image was established on Manikuta in Kamarupa as Hayagriva Madhava.

The Cult of Vishnu reached South India quite early. Early Tamil works of Sangam period speak of popularity of Vishnu worship in Tamil country. Shilappadhikaram mentions Vishnu temples of the region. Apart from Vengadam it speaks of Srirangam temple, Arankam.

A Brahmin pilgrim thus speaks about the Srirangam temple: 'I came to satisfy my heart's desire, to see with my own eyes the glory of Vishnu whom many worships with prayers as he reposes with Lakshmi on his breasts, on the couch of the thousand-hooded serpent, in the temple of Turutti (islet) jutting out on the widening waves of Kaveri, even as the blue clouds repose supine on the slopes of lofty golden mountain (meru)'.

He further says: 'If you do not take that route, but choose the route to the left, you would hear winged beetles singing the tune of sevvali in the low lying fields, in glades with cool flowers, and in jungles, primarily desert region. Passing these you reach Tirumalkunram (the hill sacred to Vishnu, hill near Madura) that opens into a cave which removes all delusion.' According to some authorities this place was noted for the worship of Vasudeva and Balarama (The Shilappadhikaram, Dikshitar, p. 196).

Kanchi is one of the ancient cities of South India as one of the great centres of learning and habited by number of religious cult. Ashoka built a Stupa here which was later described by Chinese pilgrim Hiuen-Tsang. In the second century B.C. Patanjali in his Mahabhashya, referred to it.

There are number of Vishnu temples in Kanchi. Vishnu temple at Vehka was well known in Sangam period. Alwar Bhakti movement ensured the growth of Vaishnavite temples in South India. The magnificent Lord Varadaraja Vishnu temple at Kanchi has 'played a remarkable part in fostering the growth of Sri-Vaishnavism and has justly be ranked with the famous temples of Trirangam and Tirupati as the holiest of the holies.'

It is believed that the temple had a modest beginning in the 7th century A.D. Around the middle of 11th century there was spurt in temple building activity. By the end of 13th century the temple was nearly complete with number of subsidiary structures in place. It became one of the largest Vishnu temples of South India, having shrines for different forms or aspects of Vishnu.

The Sthalapurana, Hastigiri Mahatmyam, narrated interesting legends about the origin of the temple. Once upon time Lord Brahma performed Yajna here. Lord Vishnu emerged from the Yajna fire in the form of Varadaraja. Brahma requested him to remain forever at the spot where he performed Yajna to bless his devotees for all time to come. Vishnu agreed and the temple became his abode.

The story of Gajendra Moksha, deliverance of elepants from the clutches of crocodile who caught his feet in a tank with an intension to kill him got associated with the Varadaraja temple. These legends became the themes of many devotional compositions. K.V. Raman in his Varadarajaswami Temple says that 'The legends have inspired a few festivals that are introduced in a temple and quite a few sculptural compositions found in the Kalyana Mandapa of the temple.' (p. 9)

According to Puranic legends Lord Vishnu personally stays at two places on the earth for the benefit of his devotees. One is a hill known as Vekantachalam or Venkatagiri, also known as Mudaladri Sheshachal, which is located in Chandragiri taluk of Chittur district of Andhara Pradesh and another is Puri on the sea-shore of Orissa which is the part of ancient Purushottam Kshetra, meaning Land of Vishnu.

In Andhara he is known by different names such as Venkateshvara, Shrinivasa or in popular parlance Balaji of Giri. In Puri he stays in a magnificent temple as a Jagannatha or Lord of Universe. Puranas have written about both the places and their sacred places. Skanda Purana speaks of both of them in details.

Since ancient times Venkatachalam was known to devouts as one of the most sacred places and centres of pilgrimage. The Bhagavata Purana says that Balarama, elder brother of Krishna, visited it when he set out on pilgrimage. Bhagavata says : Dravideshu mahapunyam drishvadrim venkatam prabhu. For Venkatachalam

"Bhagavata uses the epithet - Mahapunyam - that is most sacred (10.79.13).

The hill is considered as the form of Shesha Naga or great serpent Shesha on whose coils Vishnu sleeps in the milky ocean.

Yet another legend says that once Vayu, god of winds, tried to enter the bed chamber of divine couple, Lakshmi and Vishnu. Adi Shesha who was guarding the entrance stopped Vayu from entering the bed-chamber. To test each others prowess a plan was devised. Adi Shesha with his powerful thousand hood firmly encircled the heavenly mountain Meru firmly and challenged Vayu to move it with all his might. Vayu started blowing terribly but the mountain did not budge. This fierce contest affected the population of three worlds. They approached the Adi Shesha, more powerful of the two, to let Vayu have the satisfaction of winning. Adi Shesha just for a moment lifted one of his thousand hoods by which he held the mountain firmly. Vayu had his chance and he blew away a portion of mountain with force. It fell on the earth and came to be known as Sheshachalam.

Venkatachalam means the hill that burns away all sins. According to a legend a great sinner named Madhava once visited this hill who had committed several sins including staying with a low caste whore for twelve years. When he stood on the hill all his sins were burnt away. In the next birth he was born as a son of a Chola king and ruled over Tondai Mandalam. Because the sin burning power of the hill it came to be known as Venkatachalam.

In the Skanda Purana's Vaishnava Khanda we find a chapter named Venkatachala Mahatmya in which we find the legend as to how Lord Vishnu came to stay on the Venkatachala and his marriage with Padmavati, beautiful daughter of Akashraj.

The Skanda purana says that in the Satyayuga of Vaivaswata Manvantara Vayu, the wind god, performed severe penance. Bhagavan Vishnu, with his consorts Sridevi and Bhudevi, came from heaven to bless him and stood on the bank of Swami Pushkarani, on Venkatachalam.

Later Maharshi Agastya went there and performed penance for twelve long years. He requested Vishnu to reside on the hill for ever giving darshan to his devotees.

Once upon a time king Mitravarma had a son from his beautiful wife who was named as Akasha. Akasha by his valour became Chakravarti Samrat. He married princess Dharani born in Shaka clan.

One day he decided to perform Yajna and for that he ploughed a land on the bank of river Aarani. Suddenly there appeared from the earth a girl sleeping on the bed of lotus flowers. With great joy the King adopted her. She was named as Padmavati, the lotus girl.

One day young and beautiful princess Padmavati with her friends went to collect flowers in the forest. While they were busy collecting flowers, there came a handsome man of dark complexion riding a white stallion. He was none else but Lord Vishnu himself. He fell in love with bewitching young beauty who too was attracted towards him.

Vishnu sent a marriage proposal to Akasha Raj which was immediately accepted as it came from Devadhideva Bhagvavan Narayana residing on Venkatachala. The marriage was celebrated with great pomp and show.

Bhavishya Purana has some other story to tell.

A Brahmin named Madhava used to live in the place called Kalahasti. He fell in love with a prostitute and started living with her. In her company he started eating meat and drinking liquor. After the death of the prostitute Madhava, along with a group of pilgrims, went to visit Venkatachala. As soon as he reached there all his sins were burnt out. Brahma appeared before him and told him that one of his next births will be that of a king by name Akasha Raja and he would rule over Tondamandala.

Once upon a time Rishi Kashyapa along with other sages were performing Yajna on the bank of river Janavi. They could not decide as to which deity was apt to receive the Yajna-phala. Hence they deputed Bhrugu Rishi to explore the matter.

Rishi Bhrugu went to Brahmaloka and then Kailasa but did not find Brahma or Shiva suitable for receiving the fruits of Yajna. So he proceeded to Vaikuntha. There he found Vishnu reposing on the bed of coils of serpent Shesha, Lakshmi massaging his feet. This sight made Bhrugu angry and he delivered a kick on the chest of the Lord.

This did not infuriate Vishnu. On the contrary he politely asked the sage if his feet was hurt. Pleased by this Bhrugu declared Vishnu as the best among the gods, Lakshmi following him.

But Lakshmi did not at all liked the impudent behaviour of Bhrugu Rishi. She rebuked Vishnu for tolerating such a rude behaviour. In a fit of anger she left Vishnu and went to stay in Karavir Kshetra.

Vishnu could not bear the absence of Lakshmi. He went to Venkatachala and started living in an ant-hill on the bank of a water reservoir.

After the lapse of one thousand years Chola country was blessed with a pious king. To test him one day Brahma, Rudra and Lakshmi took the forms of a cow, calf and cowherd woman respectively. Lakshmi sold the cow and the calf to Chola king. Both the animals were included in the royal herd of cows.

While grazing on the Venkatachala the cow often went to the place where Vishnu was staying in ant-hill and drench it with her milk. When the keeper of the herd noticed that everyday the udder of the particular cow was found to be devoid of milk, he followed her next day. When he saw the cow emptying her udder on the ant hill he became furious and hit her with the stick in his hand. Vishnu came forward and took the blow on his body. Instantly the cruel keeper of herd died.

Learning this Chola king rushed to the spot where all this happened. Srinivasa Vishnu told him that after suffering for some time he will be born as a Akasha Raja and he would marry his daughter Padmavati.

Vishnu then sought the permission from Varaha-Vishnu to stay on Venkatachala. One day he saw beautiful Padmavati, daughter of Akasha Raja and desired to marry her.

But all along Vishnu pined for Lakshmi. He asked the sun-god Surya to meet her in Karavira kshetra and bring her back to him. Lakshmi came with him to Venkatachala and met her Lord. He told her about his desire to marry Padmavati. Lakshmi agreed to that and Vishnu Venkateshvar married the princess Padmavati.

This basic story is narrated with number of variations and with addition of some interesting myths. According to one version Srinivasa married Padmavati without the knowledge of Lakshmi. Lakshmi quarrelled with her Lord who passified her by narrating the stories of previous births of Padmavati hinting that their marriage was inevitable.

A folk element is introduced in the story in the form of Kuruthy woman whose profession was of telling fortunes. After seeing Padmavati and falling in her love Srinivasa wanted to know about her. So in the guise of Kuruthy woman he went to the capital city of her father. When he came to know that Padmavati was daughter of the king he went to her palace. He was glad to learn that Padmavati too was suffering from love pangs. He told the king that the young man she saw in the forest was none else but Mahavishnu himself and he should immediately arrange their marriage.

Lakshmi is carved on the chest of the stone image of Venkateshvara or Srinivasa. In the east at the distance of about three kilometres from his temple at the place known as Thiruchanur is a magnificent temple of Padmavati. According to local custom the devotes visiting the Venkateshvara temple on his return must visit the temple of Padmavati. It is believed that after his temple is closed for night Lord Venkateshvara goes to the temple of Padmavati to meet her.

Yet another interesting legend says that Srinivasa borrowed gold and money from Kubera for his marriage on the promise that he would repay the debt in the Kaliyuga. Brahma and Shiva stood as witnesses to the deal in the form of two Pipal trees on the bank of a pond. They can still be seen at Tirumala.

It is said that the first temple of Venkateshvara was built in the first century A.D. T.K.T. Viraraghavacharya writes in his History of Tirupati (Vol. 1) : 'Then there is the story that the first temple of Sri Venkateshvara was built by one Tondaiman Chakravarthi who was the ruler of this part of country in the early years of the Kali Yuga. The sermise of the historical research workers is that the first Chola king of Tanjore, Karkala, had an extra-marital connection with a Naga princess; and the offspring was one Adondai, who founded the Tondaimandalam and was known as Tondaiman Chakravarty. Before he built the temple, the Deity was covered over by an ant-hill and cows used to go to the top of the ant-hill and automatically empty the milk from the udder. It was only when the phenomenon was noticed that ant-hill was opened out and the discovery made. So according to this story of the Brahmanda Purana, Thiruvengadamudaiyan's existence was discovered only in Chola Karikala's time, somewhere about the first century A.D. (p. 24)

The 'Tamil Epic Cilappatikaram refers to the hill named Venkatam in its 9th canto titled as Katukan Katai. Describing the hill and the idol of Vishnu standing upon it a Brahmin charater say: '(I also came to see) the beauty of the red-eyed Lord, holding in His beautiful lotus-hands the discus which is death to his enemies, and also milk-white conch: (to see him) wearing a garland of tender flowers on His breasts and draped in golden flowers, and dewelling on topmost crest of the tall and lofty hill named Venkatam, with innumerable waterfalls, standing like a cloud in its natural hue, adorned with rainbow and attired in lightening, in the midst of a place both sides of which are illuminated by the spreading rays of the sun and the moon.'

Commenting on this passage T.K.T. Viraraghava Charya in his History of Tirupati says : 'If, as is evident from the description that the sun and the moon illuminated the deity it must be either that there was no covering over the idol or that the covering was of pavilion type. The pavilion or Mantapam would, have been of stone or wood.' (p. 92)

Prof. V.R. Ramachandra Dikshitar who had translated the epic into English ascribes it to second century A.D. This may mean that the Mantapam described in the epic was the one raised by Tontaiman Chakravarthi in the first century A.D.

When the Alwars, Tamil Vaishnava saints, ascribed to the period between sixth and ninth centuries A.D. started singing the praise of Lord of the Tiruvengadam hill the place became famous. Nammalwar (9th century A.D.) wrote: 'Let all those who groan under the load of past Karmas, only recite Name of Vengadatturaivar (He who lives on Vengadam hill) and all their past Karmas and what they may happen to commit in this life will be completely burnt. This is satyam. By so doing they will only be acquiring good to themselves. This spacious Tiruvengadam Hill will ensure for us Moksham (liberation from the cycle of death and birth).'

Vengadam hill was considered so sacred by the Alwar saints that they it is said, did not touch it with their feet that is they never climbed over it. It is said that Saint Ramanuja (12th century A.D.) climbed it on his knees.

It is believed that basic temple structure over the Vishnu idol was constructed in the early years of tenth century A.D). Subsequently it was enlarged by adding to it more structures over years. Most of the present temple building with all its Gopuras took shape by 16th-17th centuries A.D. Viraraghava Charya wrote : 'The history of this temple in its earlier days was shaped by great men who were imbubed with Alwars' high and practical philosophy. Its fame rose by leaps and bounds. To-day this temple stands pre-eminently the greatest in the land.'

Venkatesha samo devo na bhuto na bhavishyati (Nor in the past nor in future there was and will be any god like Venkatesha) says a line repeated every day during Mantrapushpam at the temple.

In the Maharashtra and Karnataka Lord Vishnu anpeared in the form of god Vitthala. Linguistically speaking the Canarese Apabrahrnasha form of Vishnu, the Sanskrit word, is Bitti. The word Vitthala is derived from the word Bitti. In the copper-plate inscription of Shake 1171 found at village Bendegiri in Belgaon district of Karnataka,Vitthala is clearly referred to as Vishnu.

Vitthala is worshipped as Krishna also. Saint-poet Ekanatha in his poetic composition, Abhanga, wrote that Krishna, prince of Dwaraka, came to see his devotee named Pundalika, accompanied by the herd of cows and their keepers, Gopalas, to pandharpur and stayed there forever.

The name of Vitthala's consort is Rukmai or mother Rukmini for the devotees. Rukmini was Vishnu's wife in his Krishna incarnation.

The popular belief is that it was Bhakta Pundalika who was the harminger of Vitthala cult in Maharashtra. Dr. R,G. Bhandarkar in his Vaishnavism, Shaivism and Minor Religious Systems have given an interesting legend about the arrival of Krishna in Maharashtra.

The region around the present day Pandharpur was once a forest land named Dindiravana. There lived a man named Pundalika who was devoted to his old parents and served them sincerely. This pleased Krishna immensely and he decided to visit him someday.

In the meanwhile, while living in his capital city Dwaraka on sea-shore Krishna, one day, intently remembered his cowherd companion Radha of Vrindavana. When Radha, through her innate cognitive power, came to know about Krishna's desire she rushed to Dwaraka and as a gesture of intense love sat on his lap.

When Rukmini, his lawfully wedded wife, saw this she became furious and left Dwaraka and wandering about reached Dindiravana. Krishna rushed after to console her. He could persuade Rukmini to pardon him. When Krishna found out that he was not far away from the place where Pundalika lived with his parents he went to see him. That time Pundalika was massaging the feet of his parents and had no time to attend his divine guest. He threw a pair of bricks at him and asked him to stand on them till he finished his task of serving his parents. And it is said that since that time Krishna in the form of Vitthala is standing at that place. Rukmini too joined him and shrine grew around them and the place became famous as Pandharpur on the bank of river Chandrabhaga, also known as Bhima or Bhimarathi.

Vitthala image in Pandharpur shrine is in standing position with hands on the hips and elbow out. There is a high cap on his head, which according to some is Shiva linga. He is wearing fish-shaped ear-ornaments and around his neck is garland of Kaustubha jems. On his chest there are two depressions known as Srivatsalanchana and Sriniketan. He is wearing waist band and ornaments on his arms and around wrists. In one hand he is holding a conch. He is standing on square elevation which is called brick underneath of which is inverted lotus.

It is believed that this image belongs to Gupta period, preferably to 5th or 6th century A.D.

When exactly the temple of Vitthala was built is not known but as Dr. Bhandarkar says it certainly existed in the middle of 13th century. He writes: 'In a copper plate inscription of the reign of Krishna of the Yadava dynasty of Devagiri it is stated that Mallisetti, a general and viceroy of the king made, while engaged in a military expedition, the grant of a village in a Belgaum district at Paundarikakshetra a holy place situated on Bhimarathi, in the vicinity of god Vishnu, in the year 1171 of Saka era corresponding to 1249 A.D. Now if the Paundarikakshetra was situated on the Bhimarathi or Bhima river, it is certainly not unreasonable to suppose that it was same as Pandhari which is the alternative name of Pandharpur; and the God in whose vicinity the grant was made must have been Vitthal or Vithoba, here mentioned by his Sanskrit name (Vishnu) and not by the Canarese corruption.

In another inscription on stone existing at Pandharpur itself and dated 1192 Saka, which corresponds to 1270 A.D., Bhanu, the son of Keshava, is represented to have performed an Aptoryama sacrifice in Pandurangapura consequent of which crowds of people and Vitthala together with the gods were gretly gratified.' (Vaisnavism, Saivism and Minor Religious Systems, p. 87-88).

Though the cult of Vitthala flourished in Maharashtra, it is believed that it originated in Karnataka. It is stated in the Bharatiya Sanskriti Kosha that there is an ancient Vitthala temple at village Sogane in Simoga district of Karnataka. At a village called Ahobala in Karnataka there is an old image of Vitthal which, according to some scholars including G.H. Khare, is older than Vitthala image in Pandharpur, Maharashtra. A beautiful image of Vitthala was found at Tirupati in Andhra. Number of saint-poets of Karnataka like Purandaradas, Kanakdas, Vijaydas, Jagannatha and Chaundaras wrote poems extolling Vitthala.

In fact the Karnataka saints of Dasa order were firm devotees of Vitthala of Pandharpur. It is believed that 'the saints of Karnataka were the first to develop the cult of devotion to Vitthala and make it a faith.'

One of the most exquisite temples at Hampi, Vijayanagara is Vitthalswami temple. The construction of this temple began in the rule of Raja Krishna Deva in 1513, it was continued by his successor Achyuta Raja (1529-42) but, Percy Brown says, owing to its elaborate character was never entirely finished. It stands as a testimony of Dravidian style of architecture among the ruins of the great city.

In Maharashtra the popularity of Vitthala spread fast courtesy Varakari Sampradaya. Marathi saint poets like Jnaneshvara, Namadeva, Tukaram, etc. sang the odes to Vitthala.

There are several interesting legends about Vitthala and his relationship with his devotees. Apart from the factor of divine grace they reveal the true nature of Vaishnavas and Varkaris.

Damajipanta Mangalvedhekar was Kamvisdar, a revenue officer in the employ of Patshah of Vijapur. The people of his region suffered from terrible famine known in the history as Durgadevi cha dushkal. Kind hearted Damaji unlocked the government granaries under his supervision and allowed the suffering people to carry home the foodgrains without making any payment. When Padshah came to know about it he asked his Kamvisdar to pay in cash the price of the foodgrain taken away by poor and hungry population. It was impossible for Damajipanta to pay such a large sum of money. Angry Patshah pronounced death sentense for Damajipanta and asked his soldiers to capture him and bring to his court for the execution of the punishment.

Damajipanta was great devotee of Vitthala. The legend says that god Vitthala himself in the guise of Damajipanta's servant, Vithu Mahar, went to the court of Padshah and paid in gold coins, Moharas, all the money due to him.

Janabai was maid servant in the house of Saint Jnaneshvar. She composed many Abhangas, devotional poems, extolling Vitthala. The legend says that when Janabai used to feel tired working,Vitthala would come to her rescue and shared the load of her work.

Namadeo was another famous saint-poet devoted to Vitthala. The legend says that on the Dipavali day he went to the temple of Vitthala and holding him by his hand brought him home and celebrated all Dipavali rituals with him. This legend finds mention in one of the Abhagas of Janabai. It is believed that Vitthala in Pandharpur temple used to eat Prasad food fed to him by Namadeva.

Devotees of Vitthala believed that he is everywhere in all animate and inanimate objects. One day when Namadeo was taking food a dog came by and ran away with his chapati or wheat bread. Namadeo ran after him with katori of ghee in his hand. He urged the dog to allow him to put ghee on his dry chapati. He felt that if he ate chapati without ghee his stomach will be upset. He believed that Vitthala in him would suffer due to his folly of eating dry chapati.

It is said that saint Ekanatha once carried Ganga water in the kavad from Kashi to take it to his native town to bath the god as was the custom those days. While passing through a patch of desert land on his way back home he saw a thursty donkey dying for the want of water. Kind hearted Ekanatha gave all the Ganga-water in his kavad to donkey for him to quench his thurst.

It is said that pleased by his act Vitthala himself appeared before him and blessed him.

Vitthala does not only stood in his temple at Pandharpur but, according to legends mingled with his devotees sharing their pains and pleasure. Vitthala can be described as 'god of the poeople.'

Srirangam, probably the largest Vishnu temple in India, is situated in Tamilnadu. It has seven Prakaras or enclosures and number of Gopurams on entrance gates in them. In the sanctum of central temple there is a huge image of Sriranganatha-Vishnu reclining on the coils of many-hooded serpent, Shesha Naga. Once for a time Lord Narayana himself gave his auspicious image to Brahma. According to local legend Ishvaku, son of Manu, obtained from Brahma the same sacred image of Sriranganatha by performing severe penance. He established it in the city of Ayodhya. Since then he became the family deity of ruling Ishvaku dynasty. It is said that in the Tretayuga Chola king Dharmavarma went to Ayodhya to attend the Ashvamedha Yajna of king Dasharatha. There he saw the image of Sriranganatha. He desired to have it in his own kingdom. After returning from Ayodhya king Dharmavarma started performing severe penance to obtain the image. But the Rishis persuaded him to relinquish his tapas. They told him that Sriranganatha himself desires to come and live in his kingdom on the bank of river Kaveri.

When, after killing Ravana, Rama returned to Ayodhya he was coronated with great pomp and show. Bhibhishana, king of Lanka, who attended coronation ceremony was given the image of Sriranganatha by Rama. While on his way to Lanka he stopped at Chandrapushkarini on river Kaveri. He placed the image of Sriranganatha on a platform. When, after spending a few days there, Bhibhishana decided to proceed to Lanka. But when he tried to lift the image from the platform it would not budge. God wished to stay there itself on the bank of river Kaveri. The local Chola king too desired the same.

Helpless Bibhishana, sensing the divine wish, left the image then and there and proceeded to Lanka.

Vaishnava Alwar saints composed poems in praise of Ranganatha. In the 10th century Nathamuni who himself was a composer and musicologist instituted the practice of singing Alwar poems, Divya Prabandham, at Srirangam temple.

Association of Andal with Srirangam temple is a matter of great legend. Andal was only one female saint among the twelve Alwars of Tamilnadu. Different dates are ascribed to her. It is said that another Alwar saint named Periyalvar living in Srivilliputtur found her lying in Tulsi bush in a garden. He brought up the child as his own. Andal thus grew up in the Vaishnava household and pined to become the bride of the Lord.

It was a practice of Periyalvar to collect the flowers from his garden every morning and made garlands out of them to decorate the icon of the Lord in local temple.

But before the garlands reached the temple Andhal would wear those in her hair and look into the mirrior to see if she was looking beautiful enough to please him.

One day Periyalvar noticed this and was aghast at the sacrilage Andal committed. He made fresh garlands that day and put them on the icon. But the Lord who appeared in the dream of Periyalvar told him that he preferred the garlands worn by Andal.

Lord asked the Periyalvar to take the girl who considered herself as Lord's bride, to Srirangam. There she climbed the coils of Adi Shesha and merged in the icon of Ranganatha.

Passionate poems of Andal and other Alvar saints about Krishna find their echo in the Bhagavata Purana, another Vaishnava work coming from South India.

In the India's Himalayan region Vishnu lives as Badrinatha. The temple is situated on the Narayana mountain on the bank of river Alaknanda. It is said that once upon a time dence forest producing Badri-fruits covered the mountain. King Vishala once performed severe penance here. Hence this place is known as Badri-Vishala also.

In the puranic literature this sacred place is described as tapsya-sthali of Rishis Nara and Narayana. Devi Bhagavata says that they were partial incarnations of Srihari. When Indra sent god of lust Kamadeva his associate

Vasanta ritu and numerous Apsaras to disturb their tapas, Rishi Narayana created exquisitely beautiful Apsara, Urvashi, who put them all to shame.

The importance of Badarikshetra, Badarikshetra Mahima, is described in the Skanda Purana. The Purana says that Bhagavan Vishnu himself resides here. Bhagavan Agnideva, god of fire, performed penance here to get rid of sins of devouring all sorts of objectionable things.

According to local legend, recorded in Kalyan Tirthanka, the image of four armed Badarinatha-Vishnu carved out of Shaligram stone was recovered by gods from Naradakunda of river Alaknanda. Devarshi Narad became the chief priest at Badarinatha temple.

When Buddhists in the region became powerful they established their control over the temple. When they came to know that Adya Shankaracharya is coming to reclaim the temple, they threw the image in the Alakananda. Adya Shakaracharya recovered the image from the river and established it in the temple.

But when the pilgrims stopped coming to worship Badarinatha, the priest serving the temple threw it in the tapta-kunda or hot-water pit. It was reclaimed again by Ramanujacharya or one of his disciples.

In the epics and Puranas Badridham is frequently mentioned as most sacred place of Vishnu.

Deep down south, in the beautiful land of Kerala, Vishnu lives as Padmanabha Anantashayanam in a magnificent temple at Trivandrum. Here reclining image of Vishnu on the coils of serpent is the largest of its kind in India.

In the Puranas this region was known as Anantavanam. Devakarmuni who was great devotee of Vishnu built a temple here and placed in it a wooden image of Padmanabhaswami - Vishnu reclining on the coils of Shesha Naga. This temple and image, after being very old, was rennovated. In 1049 A.D. the present temple was built.

K.R. Srinivasan in his Temples in South India writes: 'Another large and important temple complex in the south of Kerala is the Padmanabhaswami, or Anantashayanam Temple, in Trivandrum, which was wholly reconstructed in the last two centuries. The stone built central shrine is appropriately oblong on plan to enshrine the reclining form of Anantashayin Vishnu. It is two storeyed with pent and gable-roof patterns for its storeys. The walls are painted and there are subsidiary shrines for deities like Krishna, Kshetrapala, Narasimha, Sasta, Garuda, etc. The open pillared Mandapa round the complex: with stone pillars, and the eastern Gopura of stone body and brickwork superstructure are in the style of Tamilnadu temples, while a subsidiary entrance to the north of the Gopura is in the traditional Kerala pattern with a gable-roof and kilivasal nasikas. (p. 186).

At Puri in Orissa Vishnu lives as Purushottama-Jagannatha, at Venkatagiri in Andhra as Srinivasa, at Pandharpur in Maharashtra as Vitthala, at Srirangam in Tamilnadu as Ranganatha, at Trivandrum in Kerala as Padmanabha, at Kanchi as Varadarajswami, at Hajo in Assam as Hayagriva Madhava in Himalayas as Badrinatha.

However some of these deities assimilated in them the shades of Vasudeva-Krishna, the most popular form of divine Vishnu.

The Bhagavata Purana includes the name of Rishabha, a Tirthankara and founder of Jain religion in the list of Vishnu's incarnations. To establish the religion of shramanas, the sky-clothed mendicants and ascetics Vishnu became the son of king Nabhi and his wife Merudevi by name Rishabha, says the Purana.

Rishabha is described as Yogeshvara, king among the Yogis. Once Indra, out of sheer jealousy, stopped the rain from falling in the Ajanabhakhanda. Laughing at Indra's foolishness Rishabha, by the power of his Yogamaya brought the rain to his country.

After spending some time in the Gurukula became Grihasta, householder, by marrying Jayanti, daughter of Indra, and became father of one hundred sons. Bharata was the eldest among them all after whose name Ajanabhakhanda became Bharatvarsha.

Rishabha was a benevolent king who ruled the kingdom observing the tenets of Dharma. Once while travelling he reached the country named Brahmavarta. Here he delivered sermons on religion to educate his sons and people. He performed one hundred Yajnas during his rule.

Gradually Rishabha discarded worldly ties and became ascetic. He even discarded his cloths and became Avadhuta. So great was his tapas that all the siddhis, occult powers, stood before him with folded hands but he refused to accept them.

Wendering around like a mad person he went to many countries of Karnataka. One day while moving in the forest of Kutakachala fire broke out and he died caught in it's fury.

The Bhagavat, says that foolish king Arhat of Konka, Venka, Kutaka under the influence of the age of Kali, without understanding the true nature of Rishabha's spiritual quest, in the name of following him, started propagating false doctarine and introduced the practices like not taking bath, discarding achamana, remaining dirty, plucking hair and started abusing Veda, Brahmin and Yajnapurusha. He led the people on Avaidiks path or path not adhering to Vedic religion.

As Jainism and Buddhism grew along with more older Bhagavatism they influenced each other. D.C. Sirkar in the Cultural Heritage of India writes:

'Jainism shares the doctrine of Ahimsa, non-violence, with Bhagavatism and Buddhism and is permeated with the influence of Hinduism, especially of Krishna cult. The Jains regarded Vasudeva and Baladeva as two of their sixtythree Salaka-purushas who are believed to be directors of the course of the earth. The legends of Mahavira's birth as known from Jain mythology, again appeared to be modelled on those of Krishna's birth. The later conception of twenty-four forms of Vishnu, on the other hand, was very probably imitated from twentyfour Jaina Tirthankaras. It may be noted that the Jaina Tirthankara Rishabha was regarded by some Bhagavatas as an avatara or incarnation of Vishnu. (p. 129-30)

Pruthu Vainya, the first king to rule over the earth, was considered to be an incarnation of Vishnu.

He is referred to in the Vedic literature but not as an incarnation of Vishnu. Later epics and Puranas declared him to be so. Mahabharata describes him as an eighth decendant of Vishnu who was responsible for establishing an instution of kingship.

He is given the credit of introducing the practise of cultivating the earth. He became the harminger of science of agriculture for the first time. He was also the founder of political administration, dandaniti. His capital was on the bank of river Yamuna. In the Brahmavarta on the bank of Saraswati river he performed several horse sacrifices.

The Puranas say that he milched the earth, prithvi, to obtain several goods for the welfare of humanity.

Gaya Charan Tripathi in his book Communication with God writes: 'According to legends narrated in the Puranas (e.g. Bhagavata) the first great ruler of this earth was king Pruthu who was the amshavatara (partial incarnation) of Vishnu. He was the one who made this earth plane and flat, hence habitable for human beings, by removing to a great extent its hills and hillocks and thus levelling it. He is also credited to have converged large tracts of earth into arable land so that it could be put to agricultural use. He is further believed to be the first to divert his attention towards exploitation of the wealth hidden in the depths of Vasundhara (treasure bearing) earth, like metals and minerals and also towards collection of herbs from the mountains. So intensive and all pervading were his activities that the Earth, from his time onward, was named after him and came to be known as Prithvi (feminine gender of Pruthu). (p. 398).

As Vishnu in the form of the earliest known benevolent king named Pruthu ruled over the earth, the sovereign rulers known to the history came to be identified as Vishnu or taken as his incarnation.

According to the Matsya and Bhagavata Puranas the divine sage Narada was an incarnation of Vishnu. Though there are number of stories about the birth of Narada, generally he is taken as mind-born son of Brahma who emerged from his lap. His presence is felt in epics and Puranas as a great devotee of Narayana-Vishnu. He is seen moving all over the three worlds holding a stringed musical instrument, Vina, in his hand and name of Narayana on his lips.

He was great musician and master of many subjects. He is credited with number of works such as Brihannaradiya, Narada Smriti, Jyotirnarad, Narada Purana, Narada Bhakti Sutra, etc.

Several myths about Narada are spread over epics and Puranas including his turning into woman when he tried to fathom the depth of Vishnu's Maya. The name of this immortal sage is found mentioned in the Vedic literature also.

Like Narada the great Yogi and sage Kapil Rishi is mentioned in the Puranas as an incarnation of Vishnu. The Puranas like Bhagavata, Vishnu say that Vishnu took this incarnation to propage Samkhya Shastra.

Dhanvantari, the physician of gods, who emerged from ocean when it was churned by gods and demons to obtain elixir of life, Amrita, was listed by Bhagavata Purana as one of the incarnations of Vishnu. When he emerged from waters he was holding the jar of Amrita, says Mahabharata.

He was reborn as a son of king Dhanva and became the king of Kashi. He invented the medical science which came to be known as Ashtanga Ayurveda.

According to yet another legend the science of Ayurveda was given to him by Indra. He was sent to earth from heaven for the welfare of human beings. By the blessing of Brahma he became the king of Kashi.

In the Krishna Janma Khanda of Brahmavaivarta Purana there is an interesting story of serpents attacking him and his disciples when he was on his way to Kailasha mountain, abode of Shiva.

When affected by poisonous fumes of serpents his disciples became unconscious he treated them with herbal medicines and brought them back to consciousness.

Seeing that the serpents were defeated by Dhanvantari, the serpent goddess Manasa herself came forward but the war was averted due to intervention of gods.

Scholars consider this story to be a parable with a moral that serpent bite could be cured with the help of herbal medicine and the traditional way of treating it with rituals and mantras, etc. are of no use. Dhanvantari is worshipped by the practitioners of Ayurveda. Dhanvantari Jayanti is observed as a part of Dipavali festival on the Dhanatrayodashi day which falls on Kartik Krishna 13. In the government museum of Bangalore there is an image of four-armed Vishnu ascribed to Gupta period. In his right hand a pot is shown. Interpreting it as a pot of Amrita, the image is taken as that of Vishnu in Dhanvantari incarnation. (Bharatiya Murtishastra, p. 70).

Incarnation of Vishnu as Hayagriva, god having the head of a horse, is mentioned in some works like Mahabharata, Devi Bhagavata, Bhagavata Purana as well as Vishnu, Skanda, Vamana, Agni Puranas.

As per Shanti Parva of Mahabharata two great demons Madhu and Kaitabha stole four Vedas from Bramha and entering the ocean reached the Rasatala. Bhagavan Narayana Vishnu assuming the form of Hayagriva killed the demons, by fighting with them and returned the Vedas to Brahma. Later by worshipping Hayagriva Galava Rishi of Panchala acquired the knowledge of Vedas. It is believed by Smritis that grace of Hayagriva is neccasry to become proficient in Vedas.

According to Kalika Purana Vishnu in the form of Hayagriva 'killed the demon Jarasura, Fever demon, on the manikuta hill and afterwords stayed there forever, as Hayagriva Madhava.

According to N.P. Joshi we start getting the Hayagriva images since Kushana period and they are mostly from Mathura. A few images of the same deity, ascribed to Gupta period are kept in different museums. On the Manikuta hillock near Hajo in Assam there is a magnificent temple of Hayagriva Madhava rebuilt by king Raghudeva in 1583. Hayagriva is to be worshipped with various mantras and Purusha Sukta of Rig Veda. Dr. Maheshvar Neog informs that the natis (female dancers) of Assam were associated mainly with the Shiva temples and Hajo temple of Hayagriva-Madhava and are connected with secular amusements in urban circles (Shankardeva and His Times, p. 269).

In the third Adyaya of Prathama Skandha of Shrimaddevibhagavata there is an interesting story about the Hayagriva incarnation of Lord Vishnu.

Shrimaddevibhagavata says: Once upon a time Lord Vishnu required to fight a war with demons which went on for ten thousand years. Tired of waging the war Vishnu went to his sacred abode, Vaikuntha, for some rest. There he sat in Padmasana posture resting his head on the upper end of his bow and went to sleep.

Meanwhile gods including Indra, Brahma, Shiva decided to perform a Yajna. They went to the place where Yajneshvar Bhagavan Vishu was emersed in yogic slumber. The gods were hesitant to disturb Vishnu. Then Brahma created a worm named Vamri and asked him to cut the string of the bow. The gods thought that when the insect would cut the string the bow would be straightened and Vishnu would receive a jolt and he would come out of his slumber.

But when the insect cut the string the bow straightened with tremendous force so much so that with its impact the head of Vishnu got severed from his body and fell into the sea.

The gods thought that only Brahmavidyaswarupini Bhagavati Jagadambika had powers to save them from this crisis.

On offering prayers to her by Vedas she was pleased. She told the gods through Akashavani that one day Bhagavan Sri Vishnu was sitting with his consort Lakshmi. Seeing her beautiful face he laughed joyfully. However Lakshmi thought that probably her husband thought that her face was ugly hence the mirth. Angry Lakshmi cursed him by saying that his head would fell down too.

Brahma told the gods that the curse of Lakshmi would prove to be beneficial to them. He had given several boons to a demon Hayagriva who had a head of horse. But also told him that his end would come at the hands of Hayagriva only.

After narrating this story to gods Brahma cut the head of a horse and saw to it that it was fixed on the torso of Vishnu. Now Vishnu with the head of horse came to be known as Hayagriva (one having the head of horse). He then killed the terrible demon Hayagriva.

A story about horse form of Vishnu is found in the sixth skandha of Srimaddevibhagavata.

Once upon a time Bhagavan Vishnu cursed his consort Lakshmi to become a mare. Afflicted by sorrow she left Vaikuntha and started living at a place called Suparnaksha situated on the confluence of rivers Yamuna and Tamasa on the earth.

Lakshmi started penance to please Shiva. He appeared before her along with his wife Parvati and host of Ganas. He blessed her that soon Vishnu would appear before her in the form of a horse and give her a son named Ekaveera from whom would start a Kshatriya (warrior) race named Haihaya.

After some time on the persuation of Chitrarupa, a messanger of Shiva, Vishnu assumed the form of a handsome horse. They together had a son called Haihaya who became famous as Ekaveera. He was adopted by King Turvasu, also known as king Harivarma belonging to the family of king Yayati.

In the Vedic literature Sun god is eqated with Vishnu as Aditya. In the Mahabhrata there is a story about Sun god who assumed the form of a horse to unite with his wife Samjna who was performing penance in the guise of a mare.

SELECT BIBLIOGRAPHY

Banerjee, P., Ther Life of Krishna in Indian Art, New Delhi, 1978.

Basham, A.L., Cultural History of India, New Delhi, 1974.

Bhandarkar, R.G., Vaishnavism, Saivism and Minor Religious Systems, New Delhi, 2001.

Bhattacharya, Haridas, Cultural History of India, Vol. IV, Calcutta, 1956.

Bulcke, C.S.J., Ramkatha, Allahabad, 1950.

Chaitanya, Krishna, Mahabharata, New Delhi, 1962.

Chanda, R.P., Archaeology and Vaishnava Tradition, Memoirs of Archaeological Survey of India, No. 5, 1920.

Chaturvedi, Parasurama, Vaishnava Dharma, 2nd Edition, Delhi.

Chaturvedi, Sitaram, Kalidas Granthavali, Kashi, 1957.

Coomaraswamy, A.K., Hist. of Indian and Indonesian Art, New Delhi, 1972.

Dange, S.A., Legends in Mahabharata, New Delhi.

Dange, S.A., Encyclopaedia of Puranic Beliefs and Practices, Vol. I to IV, New Delhi, 1986.

Danielou, Alain, Hindu Polytheism, London, 1963.

Das, Bhagavan, Krishna : A Study in the theory of the Avataras, Madras, 1929.

Eschmiamm A., Kulke and C.G. Tripathi, The Cult of Jagannatha and Religious Tradition of Orissa, Delhi, 1978.

Goswami, B.K., The Bhakti Cult in Ancient India, Calcutta, 1922.

Goswami, K.G., A Study of Vaishnavism, Calcutta, 1956.

Goswami, Srivatsa, Celebrating Krishna, Vrindavan.

Gupta, Manilal, Vishnu Puran, Gita Press, Gorakhpur, Samvat 2041.

Jaiswal, Suvira, The Origin and Development of Vaishnavism, Delhi, 1980.

Joshi, Mahadevashastri, Bharatiya Sanskriti Kosha, Vol. I to X, Pune.

Kinshey, D.R., The Divine Player Delhi, 1979.

M. Ghosh, Abhinayadarpan, Calcutta, 1975.

Macdonell, A.A., Vedic Mythology, New Delhi, 2002.

Misra, K.C., Cult of Jagannatha, Calutta, 1971.

Mittal, Prabhudayal, Vraj Ka Sanskritik Itihas, Mathura.

Mohapatra, G.N., Jagannatha in History and Religious Traditions of Orissa, Calcutta, 1982.

Miller, B.S., Gita Govinda, New York, 1977.

Poddar, Hanuman Prasad, Bhagavat Purana, Vol. I, II, Gita Press, Gorakhpur, Samvat 2033.

Raychaudhuri, H.C., Materials for the Study of the Early History of the Vaishnava Sect, New Delhi, 1975.

Saletore, R.N., Life in Gupta Age, Bombay, 1943.

Sharma, Kedarnath, Gita Govinda, Varanasi, 1976.

Shastri, Nolakantha and Srinivasachari, Advance History of India, New Delhi, 1970.

Singh Deo, J.P., Origin of Jagannatha Diety, New Delhi, 1991.

Sircar, D.C., Studies in the Religious Life of Ancient and Medieval India, Delhi, 1971.

Upadhyaya, Baldeva, Bhagavata Sampradaya, Kashi, 1953.

Varadpande, M.L., Krishna Theatre in India, New Delhi.

History of Indian Theatre, Vol. I, II, III

Gods, Goddesses and Demons, Gurgaon, 2008.

Vettam, Mani, Puranic Encyclopaedia, New Delhi, 1989.

Viraraghava Charya, T.K.T., History A. Tirupati. Vol. I, II Tirupati, 2003.

Vyas, Bholashankar, Dasharupaka, Varanasi, 1967.

Winternitz, M., A History of Indian Literature, Vol. I, II, New Delhi, 1977.

Zimmer, Heinrich, Myths and Symbols of Indian Art and Civilisation, 1963.

Also Vedic Literatures, epics Ramayan and Mahabharata, Puranas, Classical Sanskrit works including drama and poetry and story works like Panchatantra and Kathasaritsagara.

Index